100
GREATEST FILMS
Thrille

D1470945

RadioTimes

Published by
BBC Worldwide Limited
Media Centre 201 Wood Lane London W12 7TQ
ISBN13 978-0-9555886-5-5
First edition published in the United Kingdom 2009
Copyright © 2009 BBC Worldwide Limited

Publishing Director
KATHY DAY

Publisher
DAVID ROBINSON

Senior Production Co-ordinator
STEVE CALVER

Design by
STUART MANNING

Picture research by
OLIVIA HOWITT

Typesetting by
DAVID LEWIS XML ASSOCIATES LTD

Printed in Great Britain by
ANCIENT HOUSE PRESS PLC

Mixed Sources
Product group from well-managed
forests and other controlled sources
www.fsc.org Cert no. BV-COC-051005 FSC
© 1996 Forest Stewardship Council
FSC

Contents

Foreword by *Andrew Collins*

SOME PEOPLE SEEK THEIR THRILLS on insane, lunch-endangering rides at theme parks, or by skydiving or bungee-jumping. I get mine from watching thrillers. But what is a thriller? Allow me to define our terms, as un-thrilling as that may sound.

Firstly, an action/adventure is not necessarily a thriller. Nor is a fantasy or horror movie. All have the power to thrill – an explosion; a medieval battle between mythical beasts; a young lady in denim shorts running through the woods – but not all are thrillers. In many ways, the thriller cuts across genres. As a group, it's catholic, covering a vast waterfront of subject matter and style. *All the President's Men* is a thriller – political, based on documentary evidence and relying on phone conversations, typewriters and people knocking on doors – and so is *Psycho* (yes, there are a couple of nasty bits with a kitchen knife, but it's essentially about the impulsive theft of $40,000, and the twists and turns that occur as a result).

After seeing back-to-back trailers for *Transformers: Revenge of the Fallen, GI Joe* and *Harry Potter and the Half-Blood Prince*, director Terry Gilliam complained that he was experiencing "the same explosions . . . the same rhythms . . . it was all the same film." His slightly grumpy point about the homogeneity of modern action/fantasy blockbusters is a pertinent one. This is why focusing on the thriller genre – one that reaches back as far as the 1920s and takes in *noir*, sexual intrigue, mistaken identity, car chases and high-concept serial murder – is a useful way of distilling something more potent and subtle from the broader action-based categories.

If Alfred Hitchcock directed it, you're halfway there. (The "Master of Suspense" is responsible for 12 of our 100, including *Psycho*.) And if he might have approved – as, you'd like to think, with *Jagged Edge, Dressed to Kill, The Usual Suspects, Blood Simple* – you're probably looking at a first-class modern thriller.

Tension, in the right context, can be supplied by the relentless re-examination of a tape recording (*The Conversation*), a police interview through strengthened glass (*The Silence of the Lambs*), or the implied threat behind a repeated question (*Marathon Man's* "Is it safe?"). A cinematic thrill-ride does not have to be a CGI-heavy computer-game rip-off – what about *Speed, Deliverance*, or even *Duel*? Crime is in fact the only meaningful constant here, whether terrorist threat, bank heist, confidence trick, homicide, siege, hijack, assassination, kidnap, cover-up or auction of body parts after anaesthetic switcheroo.

If the edge of your seat is always the first part to wear out, you've come to the right place. Here's my test: if you're slumped in your armchair, it's not a thriller. ▪

Acknowledgements

REVIEWERS

ANDREW COLLINS has been the film editor of *Radio Times* since 2001. On BBC Radio 4, he presented *Back Row* and still contributes to and occasionally presents *The Film Programme*. The regular host of TCM's Short Film Awards and a former editor of *Empire* magazine, he also co-hosted ITV's *Collins & Maconie's Movie Club* with Stuart Maconie.

DAVID PARKINSON has been reviewing for *Radio Times* since 1995. Specialising in foreign-language films, he is a contributing editor on *Empire* magazine. Among his books are *A History of Film*, *Mornings in the Dark: the Graham Greene Film Reader*, *Oxford at the Movies* and *The Rough Guide to Film Musicals*.

DAVE ALDRIDGE is a former editor of *Film Review* magazine. He is currently presenter of a weekly film and DVD phone-in for BBC Radio Five Live and is a regular contributor to *Radio Times* and other entertainment magazines.

JO BERRY has written about film for publications including *Empire*, *eve*, *Maxim*, *Sight & Sound*, *The Guardian* and the *Daily Express*. She is author of *The Ultimate DVD Easter Egg Guide*, *Chick Flicks* (with Angie Errigo) and *The Parents' Guide to Kids' Movies*.

JASON CARO is a devotee of sci-fi, fantasy and thrillers, and has been a regular contributor to *Film Review* magazine as well as several specialist science-fiction publications.

JOHN FERGUSON has edited video and DVD magazines in the UK and Australia, including *Video Home Entertainment* and *Video Retailer*, most recently serving as editor of the Melbourne-based *Screen Print*. He is now based in New Zealand where he is setting up a new online DVD publication.

SLOAN FREER is an arts journalist and film critic with a passion for leftfield cinema. She has contributed to publications including *The Observer*, *Q*, *Total Film*, *Metro*, *Kerrang!* and *Bizarre*.

LORIEN HAYNES is a freelance film journalist and broadcaster, who has reviewed and interviewed for *The Observer*, *Elle*, *Red*, *Woman's Hour*, *You and Yours*, *The Green Room* and *GMTV*.

TOM HUTCHINSON, who sadly died in August 2005, contributed film reviews to *Radio Times* for a decade, and also wrote for *The Sunday Telegraph*, *The Mail on Sunday* and *Now!* magazine. A broadcaster for both radio and film, he also worked with director J Lee Thompson on several scripts, and wrote books on Marilyn Monroe and his friend Rod Steiger.

ALAN JONES has reviewed for *Radio Times* since 1995. He has written numerous TV programmes, including two documentaries on the Italian horror directors Mario Bava and Dario Argento, and is the author of *The Rough Guide to Horror Movies*.

ROBYN KARNEY is a former critic and interviewer for *Empire* magazine. Her books include *The Foreign Film Guide* with Ronald Bergan, *A Star Danced: the Life of Audrey Hepburn* and *A Singular Man: Burt Lancaster*.

STELLA PAPAMICHAEL is a freelance journalist who has reviewed films since her teens. She contributes to *Total Film* magazine and was a regular reviewer for bbc.co.uk/movies.

BRIAN PENDREIGH is a former cinema editor of *The Scotsman* and currently writes for a range of publications in the UK and overseas, including *The Times* and *Herald*. He won the Ainsworth Film Journalist of the Year award in 1995 and 1999.

TONY SLOMAN is a producer, editor and writer. His credits include *Radio On*, *Cross of Iron*, *Chitty Chitty Bang Bang* and cult TV series *The Prisoner*. A lecturer and broadcaster, he served for ten years as a governor of the BFI and is a life member of Bafta.

ADAM SMITH was deputy editor of *Empire* between 1997 and 2000, and remains the magazine's Senior Features Writer. He is also a freelance journalist and has written about movies for *Q*, *GQ*, *FHM*, *Arena*, *The Observer* and *The Independent*, and is a regular contributor to Radio 4's *Front Row*.

ADDITIONAL REVIEWERS

Leslie Felperin, Peter Freedman, Sue Heal, David McGillivray, John Marriott, David Oppedisano, Simon Rose, Adrian Turner

EDITORIAL TEAM

Edited by **SUE ROBINSON**, **COLIN PRIOR**
Contributing editor **ANDREW COLLINS**
Radio Times Film Unit **JEREMY ASPINALL**, **LUCY BARRICK**, **TOM FOLLEY**, **JAMIE HEALY**, **TONY PETERS**, **CAROLINE MARTIN**
Additional writing/research **SUSANNAH STRAUGHAN**, **ANNA RICHARDS**, **RUPERT FROST**, **PAUL BUTLER**, **STEVE MORRISSEY**, **CARI THOMAS**
Marketing by **PAUL CUMISKEY**, **TOM GUNN**
Database designed by **MARK GINNS**

PICTURE ACKNOWLEDGEMENTS

All pictures were sourced from a variety of picture libraries and suppliers, as listed below. For details of the copyright holder/s on each picture, please contact the supplier.
ABSOLUTE FILM ARCHIVE pp60, 124, 150
ALLSTAR pp1-12, 18-44, 48-58, 64, 68-74, 78-82, 86, 88, 92-98, 102-116, 120, 122, 126, 130-148, 152-162, 166-172, 176-186, 190-198, 202-208, 214, 215a, 216, 217, 218
KOBAL COLLECTION pp14, 16, 46, 62, 66, 76, 84, 90, 118, 128, 164, 174, 188, 210, 215b
MOVIESTORE COLLECTION p200
PHOTO12 p100

SOURCES

Certain data published under licence from Baseline II Inc.
Certain data published under licence from the British Board of Film Classification.
Some material is verified from the Motion Picture Guide, published by Cinebooks, New York, with kind permission.

Introduction

Welcome to the Radio Times 100 Greatest Films series, a set of books to collect and treasure that provides a lively, colourful and informative guide to *the* 100 movies in key genres. In this case, it's thriller, from the 1930s (*The 39 Steps*) through to the latest critical or commercial successes (*The Bourne Trilogy*). We invite you to join us in our love of cinema, as we celebrate the best films of their kind throughout the history of the moving image, with detailed entries for each film in the 100 as well as expert analyses at the back of the book on the key influences – director, musical score – in each genre. You can use these books to enhance your knowledge of film, to have fun testing your friends and family, as a starting point for your own list, or even to build a comprehensive DVD or Blu-ray library.

And how did we come up with the 100? Well, fierce debate and noisy deliberation played a major part. But the nuts and bolts of the process were that all contributors voted for their top 50 in the genre, each top ten was allocated points (from 12 down to 3), with the remaining 40 getting 1 point apiece. These points were then weighted according to how many times a film had been voted for, ensuring that no one person's tastes would outweigh the majority. The points were collated and the results are before you.

Honourable mention must go to the films that almost made the 100 – but not quite. *Midnight Run* was a popular choice, yet got more votes as a comedy, while *LA Confidential* got strong backing as a thriller, yet fell at the last hurdle, with the majority putting it firmly in the crime drama camp. The **Contributors' Top Tens** section at the back of the book is marked with asterisks against titles that are not in the 100, to give you a flavour of the films that were considered but didn't make the list.

ENTRY DETAILS Every entry includes a plot synopsis and a review providing critical insights from our expert writing team (see left). ● The most memorable line from each film is quoted, with behind-the-scenes anecdotes about the film and its stars. ● We also list the essential technical details, starting with the film's British Board of Film Classification certificate (U – suitable for all; PG – parental guidance; 12, 15, 18 – passed for people of these ages and over). ● Please note that many of these films will not be suitable for family viewing, and you should be guided by the certificate and content advice when deciding on a film's suitability. ● Other details include major cast and director/writing credits. Some actors/directors are occasionally credited in different ways on different films. In these cases, we have printed the name as credited on that film, followed in square brackets by the name under which that person is more commonly known. ● The year quoted is the year the film was copyrighted. ● Its country (or countries) of origin (the nationality of its production companies, rather than where it was made) is also listed, and whether it is colour or black and white – or both, plus its running time. ● Major awards for each title (Oscars and Baftas) are also given, and any DVD extras are listed with details of the DVD edition being highlighted and Blu-ray availability.

If you have any changes that you'd like us to incorporate into the next edition of this book or any future additions to the series, please get in touch. Your contributions are invaluable, and we would be delighted to hear all your comments and suggestions. You can write to us at: Radio Times Films, BBC Worldwide Ltd, MC1D4 Media Centre, 201 Wood Lane, London W12 7TQ; or email us at films.radiotimes@bbc.co.uk.

SUE ROBINSON & **COLIN PRIOR**, SERIES EDITORS

All the President's Men

CERTIFICATE: **15** | YEAR: **1976** | COUNTRY: **US** | **COLOUR** | RUNNING TIME: **132 MINUTES**

SYNOPSIS

Based on the investigation by *Washington Post* reporters Carl Bernstein and Bob Woodward, this film painstakingly reconstructs the events surrounding the most significant political scandal of the 1970s, which led to the Watergate hearings and the resignation of President Richard Nixon.

REVIEW

This Oscar-winning thriller about the burglary of the Democratic Party's Watergate headquarters in 1972 and its aftermath is one of the best movies ever made about American politics and journalism. Robert Redford and Dustin Hoffman star as the two young *Washington Post* reporters (Bob Woodward and Carl Bernstein) whose stubborn digging ultimately led to the downfall of Richard Nixon, 37th President of the United States. William Goldman's script brilliantly clarifies the multilayered labyrinth of corruption, while Alan J Pakula's tense direction draws telling parallels between the blazing white open-plan offices of the *Post* (no secrets here) and the dark murky world of Washington politics. There's great support, too, from Jason Robards as the *Post's* editor, Ben Bradlee, and Hal Holbrook as creepy informant "Deep Throat". **ADRIAN TURNER**

CAST

Robert Redford *Bob Woodward* • Dustin Hoffman *Carl Bernstein* • Jack Warden *Harry Rosenfeld* • Martin Balsam *Howard Simons* • Hal Holbrook *Deep Throat* • Jason Robards *Ben Bradlee* • Jane Alexander *Book-keeper* • Meredith Baxter *Debbie Sloan* • Ned Beatty *Dardis* • Stephen Collins *Hugh Sloan Jr*

DIRECTOR

Alan J Pakula

SCREENPLAY

William Goldman, from the book by Bob Woodward, Carl Bernstein

AWARDS

Academy Awards (4): Supporting Actor (Jason Robards), Adapted Screenplay, Art Direction, Sound

DVD EXTRAS

Special Edition: commentary by Robert Redford; two making-of featurettes; *Out of the Shadows: The Man Who Was Deep Throat* featurette; featurette on Woodward and Bernstein; vintage Jason Robards interview; Alan J Pakula thrillers trailer gallery.

CONTENT ADVICE

Contains swearing.

QUOTE UNQUOTE

How do you think your cheque got into the bank account of a Watergate burglar? **BOB WOODWARD**

IF YOU ENJOYED THIS, WHY NOT TRY . . .

The Parallax View (1974)
Three Days of the Condor (1975)

DID YOU KNOW?

"You can always ride off into the sunset in your next film, but I'm forever an asshole," was how *Washington Post* editor Ben Bradlee expressed his fears of being portrayed on screen by Jason Robards.

00:00   7:11
00:00   10
00:00   09
00:00   08
00:00   07
00:0   :06
00:0   :05
00:00   0:04
00:00   0:03
00:00   02
00:0   01

Arlington Road

CERTIFICATE: **15** | YEAR: **1998** | COUNTRY: **US/UK** | **COLOUR** | RUNNING TIME: **112 MINUTES**

CAST
Jeff Bridges *Michael Faraday* • Tim Robbins *Oliver Lang* • Joan Cusack *Cheryl Lang* • Hope Davis *Brooke Wolf* • Robert Gossett *FBI Agent Whit Carver* • Mason Gamble *Brady Lang* • Spencer Treat Clark *Grant Faraday* • Stanley Anderson *Dr Archer Scobee*

DIRECTOR
Mark Pellington

SCREENPLAY
Ehren Kruger

CONTENT ADVICE
Contains violence, swearing.

SYNOPSIS

Washington college professor Michael Faraday has lived a lonely life with his young son since his wife's death at the hands of right-wing extremists. When he begins to suspect that his new neighbours are terrorists, is he allowing his paranoia to get the better of him, or is he right to suspect them?

REVIEW

Is college professor Jeff Bridges's friendly new neighbour (played by Tim Robbins) an urban terrorist living incognito in an anonymous Washington suburb while he plans to bomb a government target? Or is that merely an outrageous theory fuelled by Bridges's fragile state of mind following the death in the line of duty of his FBI agent wife? Director Mark Pellington and screenwriter Ehren Kruger (*Transformers: Revenge of the Fallen*) audaciously chips away at the American psyche here to deliver a gripping psychological thriller, powered by totally sympathetic and believable performances from Bridges, Hope Davis as his girlfriend and Joan Cusack in a rare serious role as Robbins's wife. The suspense comes from never letting the viewer in on the supposed conspiracy theory right up to the stunning and truly shocking finale. This is seat-edge stuff, with a sobering message. **ALAN JONES**

QUOTE UNQUOTE

Never wiser than when we're children. **OLIVER LANG**

IF YOU ENJOYED THIS, WHY NOT TRY ...

The 'Burbs (1989)
Pacific Heights (1990)

DID YOU KNOW?

Director Mark Pellington won an MTV Video Music Award for directing Pearl Jam's video *Jeremy*.

A WHITE-HOT NIGHT OF HATE!

ASSAULT ON PRECINCT 13

THE GANG THAT SWORE A BLOOD OATH TO DESTROY PRECINCT 13... AND EVERY COP IN IT!

POLICE 13

IRWIN YABLANS Presents a CKK PRODUCTION "ASSAULT ON PRECINCT 13"
Starring AUSTIN STOKER

DARWIN JOSTON • LAURIE ZIMMER • Executive Producer JOSEPH KAUFMAN

 R RESTRICTED   Written and Directed by JOHN CARPENTER • PANAVISION® METROCOLOR Distributed by
©Copyright 1976 CKK Corporation   Produced by J.S. KAPLAN

Assault on Precinct 13

CERTIFICATE: **15** | YEAR: **1976** | COUNTRY: **US** | **COLOUR** | RUNNING TIME: **90 MINUTES**

SYNOPSIS

In the Los Angeles ghetto of Anderson, six young gang members are shot dead by police. Meanwhile, Lieutenant Ethan Bishop is given the easy job of caretaking the last few hours of a precinct police station that is to be closed down. But when he gives refuge to a man on the run, a nightmare begins.

REVIEW

This violent and gripping thriller from director John Carpenter is a model of low-budget film-making. A hybrid of *Rio Bravo* and *Night of the Living Dead*, it ranks as one of the best B-movies ever made in the urban horror action genre. Set in a rundown area of Los Angeles, it follows the siege of a nearly abandoned police station by a heavily armed street gang, after the arrest of the catatonic killer of the gang's fearless leader. The occupants of the under-equipped station – death-row criminals and the police – must fight together when all contact with the outside world is severed. Parts of the film – notably, the shocking ice-cream van sequence – rank among the high points of Carpenter's output; he also supplies the taut synthesiser score that adds to the eerie atmosphere of this terrific cult gem. ALAN JONES

CAST

Austin Stoker *Ethan Bishop* • Darwin Joston *Napoleon Wilson* • Laurie Zimmer *Leigh* • Martin West *Lawson* • Tony Burton *Wells* • Kim Richards *Kathy*

DIRECTOR

John Carpenter

SCREENPLAY

John Carpenter

DVD EXTRAS

Special Edition: commentary by John Carpenter; interview with John Carpenter and Austin Stoker; isolated score; production history; radio spots; original theatrical trailer.

CONTENT ADVICE

Contains violence, swearing.

QUOTE UNQUOTE

Look at that, two cops wishing me luck. I'm doomed. WELLS

IF YOU ENJOYED THIS, WHY NOT TRY . . .

Night of the Living Dead (1968)
Rio Bravo (1958)

DID YOU KNOW?

John T Chance, the editor on the movie, is a pseudonym used by John Carpenter in homage to Howard Hawks's classic 1958 western *Rio Bravo* (it's the name of John Wayne's sheriff) from which the siege-centred storyline is borrowed.

Bad Day at Black Rock

CERTIFICATE: **PG** | YEAR: **1955** | COUNTRY: **US** | **COLOUR** | RUNNING TIME: **78 MINUTES**

SYNOPSIS

In 1945, one-armed war veteran John J Macreedy arrives in the remote desert town of Black Rock and enquires where he might find a Japanese farmer called Komoko. The request creates an atmosphere of hostility and violence among the small community that rapidly puts Macreedy's life in jeopardy.

REVIEW

In this simmering suspense drama, an Oscar-nominated Spencer Tracy hits the peak of his powers as the one-armed Second World War veteran, who arrives in a small south-western town to present a Japanese farmer with his son's posthumous medal. However, the remote desert community harbours a dark secret that Robert Ryan and his fellow rednecks are prepared to do anything to protect. Howard Breslin's source story, *Bad Day at Hondo*, is essentially melodramatic. In the film, director John Sturges and cinematographer William C Mellor achieve an atmosphere of deceptive calm that makes the wait for the inevitable (and surprisingly shocking) showdown all the more tense. Tracy gives a masterclass in screen acting and Ryan is also on career-best form, while Ernest Borgnine and Lee Marvin are marvellously malevolent as Ryan's racist heavies.

DAVID PARKINSON

CAST

Spencer Tracy *John J Macreedy* • Robert Ryan *Reno Smith* • Anne Francis *Liz Wirth* • Dean Jagger *Tim Horn* • Walter Brennan *Doc Velie* • John Ericson *Pete Wirth* • Ernest Borgnine *Coley Trimble* • Lee Marvin *Hector David*

DIRECTOR

John Sturges

SCREENPLAY

Millard Kaufman, Don McGuire, from the story *Bad Day at Hondo* by Howard Breslin

QUOTE UNQUOTE

The rule of law has left here, and the guerrillas have taken over. **JOHN J MACREEDY**

IF YOU ENJOYED THIS, WHY NOT TRY ...

Shane (1953)

DID YOU KNOW?

Spencer Tracy had difficulty striking matches using one hand, as the script demanded. He eventually convinced John Sturges to let him use a lighter.

Battle Royale

CERTIFICATE: **18** | YEAR: **2000** | COUNTRY: **JPN** | **COLOUR** | RUNNING TIME: **108 MINUTES**

SYNOPSIS

In an effort to curb the descent into violent anarchy by the country's rebellious youth, the Japanese government sends a group of schoolchildren to an isolated island and gives them three days to reduce their number to a single, chastened survivor. An explosive collar makes sure they comply.

REVIEW

Kinji Fukasaku's violent film depicts an annual competition of the future in which, as a lesson to unruly youth, a class of schoolchildren are taken to an island, equipped with various weapons and given just three days to reduce their number to the sole survivor who will then be allowed to rejoin society. Each is fitted with an explosive collar to make sure they play the game – like *Survivor* but by way of *Lord of the Flies*. Based on a novel by Koshun Takami, this is a film of contrasting moods, with moments of bleak comedy and grotesque horror being interspersed with genuinely touching insights into teen trauma. It's occasionally ragged, but the characterisation is sharp – particularly Takeshi as a world-weary former teacher who monitors the teenagers' "progress" – and the murderous set pieces are often inspired. **DAVID PARKINSON**

CAST
"Beat" Takeshi [Takeshi Kitano] *Kitano* • Taro Yamamoto *Shogo Kawada, male student 5* • Masanobu Ando *Kazuo Kiriyama, male student 6* • Sosuke Takaoka *Hiroki Sugimura, male student 11* • Tatsuya Fujiwara *Shuya Nanahara, male student 15* • Hirohito Honda *Niida Yoriyuki, male student 16* • Eri Ishikawa *Yukie Utsumi, female student 2*

DIRECTOR
Kinji Fukasaku

SCREENPLAY
Kenta Fukasaku, from a novel by Koshun Takami

DVD EXTRAS
Two-disc Special Edition: making-of featurette; audition and rehearsal footage; special effects comparison featurette; behind-the-scenes and on-set featurettes; TV spots; theatrical trailer; Tokyo film festival footage; press conference; director's statement; alternative endings.

QUOTE UNQUOTE

There's a way out of this game. Kill yourselves together. Here, now. If you can't do that, then don't trust anyone. Just run! **SHOGO KAWADA, MALE STUDENT 5**

IF YOU ENJOYED THIS, WHY NOT TRY . . .

Lord of the Flies (1963)
Lord of the Flies (1990)

DID YOU KNOW?
Stunt doubles weren't used in this film – not even by the main actors – to make the action as realistically harrowing as possible.

The Big Heat

CERTIFICATE: **15** | YEAR: **1953** | COUNTRY: **US** | **BW** | RUNNING TIME: **85 MINUTES**

SYNOPSIS

When homicide detective Dave Bannion is assigned to investigate a colleague's apparent suicide, he is sceptical about the reasons given for his death. When the dead man's mistress tells him a very different version of events and is later found murdered, Bannion realises he has uncovered a conspiracy.

REVIEW

Introduced with the memorable tagline "Somebody's going to pay... because he forgot to kill me", Glenn Ford crusades against Mob-led civic corruption and hunts for vengeance in this classic *film noir* from director Fritz Lang. Its most famous scene, when moll Gloria Grahame is scalded by hot coffee hurled by crook Lee Marvin, was trimmed by the censors before the movie could be released in Britain with an X certificate. Now fully restored, it's tame by today's standards with the actual scalding occurring off-camera, but it still packs a punch. Ford is excellent as the single-minded cop who's absorbed by his mission – his character was based on the investigators who uncovered the bile in US cities during the televised 1950s Estes Kefauver Senate investigations – and Lang gives the vicious exposé a sleek and glossy surface. **TONY SLOMAN**

CAST

Glenn Ford *Dave Bannion* • Gloria Grahame *Debby Marsh* • Jocelyn Brando *Katie Bannion* • Alexander Scourby *Mike Lagana* • Lee Marvin *Vince Stone* • Jeanette Nolan *Bertha Duncan* • Peter Whitney *Tierney* • Willis Bouchey *Lt Wilkes*

DIRECTOR

Fritz Lang

SCREENPLAY

Sydney Boehm, from the serial in *The Saturday Evening Post* by William P McGivern

QUOTE UNQUOTE

Well, you're about as romantic as a pair of handcuffs.
DEBBY MARSH

IF YOU ENJOYED THIS, WHY NOT TRY . . .
American Gangster (2007)

DID YOU KNOW?

Glenn Ford's wife was played by Marlon Brando's older sister, Jocelyn. It was only her second movie, yet her screen career never really took off. However, she did appear alongside her famous brother in *The Ugly American* (1963) and *The Chase* (1966).

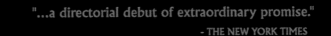

"...a directorial debut of extraordinary promise."
- THE NEW YORK TIMES

"The most inventive and original
thriller in many a moon. A maliciously
entertaining murder story."
-David Ansen, NEWSWEEK

"...a debut as scarifyingly
assured as any since
Orson Welles..."
-TIME MAGAZINE

John Getz • Frances McDormand • Dan Hedaya

BLOOD SIMPLE

Blood Simple

CERTIFICATE: **18** | YEAR: **1983** | COUNTRY: **US** | **COLOUR** | RUNNING TIME: **98 MINUTES**

SYNOPSIS

Texas bar owner Julian Marty hires sleazy private detective Loren Visser to kill his cheating wife, Abby, and her bartender lover, Ray. But instead of carrying out his assignment, Visser takes the money and kills Marty. Then Ray finds Marty's body and leaps to altogether the wrong conclusion...

REVIEW

Joel and Ethan Coen made their feature debut with this modern classic, in which a jealous Texas husband (played by Dan Hedaya) hires a sleazy private eye (M Emmet Walsh) to murder his adulterous wife (Frances McDormand) and her lover (John Getz). Blending elements of novelist James M Cain (*The Postman Always Rings Twice*), *film noir*, Hitchcock thrillers and contemporary horror movies, this dark morality tale deviates imaginatively from the 1940s murder mysteries that it evokes. The acting is first rate (the long road to McDormand's Oscar for *Fargo* started here) and the atmosphere is appropriately brooding. The Coen brothers' use of light and space is impressive, and the innovative camerawork (by *Men in Black* director Barry Sonnenfeld) to increase the suspense is breathtaking, particularly in the almost unbearably tense finale.
ALAN JONES

CAST

John Getz *Ray* • Frances McDormand *Abby* • Dan Hedaya *Julian Marty* • M Emmet Walsh *Visser* • Samm-Art Williams *Maurice* • Deborah Neumann *Debra* • Raquel Gavia *Landlady* • Van Brooks *Man from Lubbock*

DIRECTOR

Joel Coen

SCREENPLAY

Ethan Coen, Joel Coen

DVD EXTRAS

Coen brothers filmography.

CONTENT ADVICE

Contains sex scenes, violence, swearing.

QUOTE UNQUOTE

He was alive when I buried him. **BARTENDER RAY**

IF YOU ENJOYED THIS, WHY NOT TRY ...

Red Rock West (1992)

DID YOU KNOW?

Holly Hunter had to turn down a role in the Coen brothers' debut feature, so instead persuaded her room-mate, Frances McDormand, to audition for the part. McDormand ended up marrying director Joel Coen the following year.

Blow Out

CERTIFICATE: **18** | YEAR: **1981** | COUNTRY: **US** | **COLOUR** | RUNNING TIME: **103 MINUTES**

SYNOPSIS

Movie sound technician Jack Terry is making a recording when he witnesses a car accident. He manages to rescue the female passenger, but the driver, who he later learns was a leading politician, dies. When his tape reveals the sound of a gunshot, Jack begins to suspect that the crash was no accident.

REVIEW

Long before he starred in *Pulp Fiction*, John Travolta's best role was here in Brian De Palma's audio version of Michelangelo Antonioni's *Blowup*. It's laced with the director's usual quota of Hitchcockian black humour and suspense, and Travolta is marvellous as the cheesy Philadelphia-based horror flick sound-effects man who accidentally tapes a Chappaquiddick-type car accident that leads to the drowning of a presidential candidate. DePalma's then-wife Nancy Allen plays the girl that Travolta rescues from the accident, and other characters with plenty to hide include Dennis Franz's sleazy private eye and John Lithgow's sinister operative who's trying to clear up the mess. Nothing is what it seems in this paranoid mystery that's overflowing with De Palma's trademark high style and cinematic technique right up to the knockout, downbeat Liberty Bell ending.

ALAN JONES

CAST
John Travolta *Jack Terry* • Nancy Allen *Sally Badina* • John Lithgow *Burke* • Dennis Franz *Manny Karp* • John Aquino *Detective Mackey* • Peter Boyden *Sam* • Curt May *Donahue* • John McMartin *Lawrence Henry* • Deborah Everton *Hooker*

DIRECTOR
Brian De Palma

SCREENPLAY
Brian De Palma

DVD EXTRAS
Theatrical trailer.

CONTENT ADVICE
Contains violence, swearing, nudity.

QUOTE UNQUOTE

No-one wants to know about conspiracy any more!

JACK TERRY

IF YOU ENJOYED THIS, WHY NOT TRY ...

Blowup (1966)
The Conversation (1974)

DID YOU KNOW?
John Travolta's glum playing and downbeat appearance were the result of insomnia.

Blue Velvet

CERTIFICATE: **18** | YEAR: **1986** | COUNTRY: **US** | **COLOUR** | RUNNING TIME: **115 MINUTES**

SYNOPSIS

Jeffrey Beaumont's corner of small-town America is a pretty and peaceful place. But not far below the apparently idyllic surface lies a dark and violent world occupied by gangster Frank Booth and night-club singer Dorothy Vallens, upon which young Jeffrey stumbles when he discovers a severed ear.

REVIEW

This is the most complete of David Lynch's films, made before his disturbing black vision of small-town American life veered into self-parody. The dark tone is set from the opening sequence, which starts with white picket fences and cheery firemen but ends with a man suffering a stroke in his garden while insect life seethes beneath the lawn. Kyle MacLachlan (who made his acting debut for Lynch in *Dune* in 1984) plays the young innocent who gets sucked into the bizarre sadomasochistic relationship between nightclub singer Isabella Rossellini and monstrous local crime boss Dennis Hopper. The latter resurrected his career after years in the wilderness with a crazed portrait of evil – legend has it that Hopper said "I've got to play Frank. Because I am Frank." Once experienced here, listening to Roy Orbison's *In Dreams* will never be the same again. **JOHN FERGUSON**

CAST

Kyle MacLachlan *Jeffrey Beaumont* • Isabella Rossellini *Dorothy Vallens* • Dennis Hopper *Frank Booth* • Laura Dern *Sandy Williams* • Hope Lange *Mrs Williams* • Dean Stockwell *Ben* • George Dickerson *Detective Williams* • Brad Dourif *Raymond* • Jack Nance *Paul*

DIRECTOR

David Lynch

SCREENPLAY

David Lynch

DVD EXTRAS

Strange Desires documentary: includes archive interviews with David Lynch and new interviews with producer Dino De Laurentiis, star Dennis Hopper; archive review from the BBC's *Moving Pictures* series with JG Ballard; theatrical trailer.

CONTENT ADVICE

Contains violence, swearing, drug abuse, sex scenes, nudity.

QUOTE UNQUOTE

Frank... is a very sick and dangerous man. **JEFFREY BEAUMONT**

IF YOU ENJOYED THIS, WHY NOT TRY ...

Twin Peaks: Fire Walk with Me (1992)

DID YOU KNOW?

Roy Orbison initially rejected David Lynch's request to use *In Dreams*, but later made a video for the song with scenes from the film.

Body Heat

CERTIFICATE: **18** | YEAR: **1981** | COUNTRY: **US** | **COLOUR** | RUNNING TIME: **108 MINUTES**

SYNOPSIS

In a small town on the coast of Florida that's sweltering in the grip of a stifling heatwave, low-rent lawyer Ned Racine becomes embroiled in a torrid love affair with the beautiful but married Matty Walker. As Ned becomes increasingly infatuated, a plan is hatched to kill Matty's wealthy husband.

REVIEW

This dazzling directorial debut from Lawrence Kasdan (the screenwriter of blockbusters like *Raiders of the Lost Ark*) certainly packs a steamy punch. William Hurt plays the small-town lawyer who falls for *femme fatale* Kathleen Turner only to find himself ensnared in a tortuous plot to murder her wealthy husband (Richard Crenna). Kasdan respectfully tips his hat to classics such as *Double Indemnity*, but the intricate plotting and sly humour ensure that his film stands in its own right. The performances are first rate, too: Turner sizzles, while Hurt is excellent as the ordinary Joe getting increasingly out of his depth. There's also a creepy cameo from Mickey Rourke and a jolly supporting role for the then unknown Ted Danson. And special mention should go to John Barry's moody, jazz-tinged score, which is a perfect complement to the clammy action. **JOHN FERGUSON**

CAST
William Hurt *Ned Racine* • Kathleen Turner *Matty Walker* • Richard Crenna *Edmund Walker* • Ted Danson *Peter Lowenstein* • JA Preston *Oscar Grace* • Mickey Rourke *Teddy Lewis* • Kim Zimmer *Mary Ann* • Jane Hallaren *Stella* • Lanna Sanders *Roz Kraft*

DIRECTOR
Lawrence Kasdan

SCREENPLAY
Lawrence Kasdan

DVD EXTRAS
Production notes; theatrical trailer.

CONTENT ADVICE
Contains violence, swearing, sex scenes, nudity.

QUOTE UNQUOTE
You aren't too smart, are you? I like that in a man.
MATTY WALKER

IF YOU ENJOYED THIS, WHY NOT TRY . . .
Build My Gallows High (1947)
Double Indemnity (1944)

DID YOU KNOW?
To make the crew feel more at ease filming the sex scenes, the naked William Hurt and Kathleen Turner introduced themselves to everyone on the set.

Bound

CERTIFICATE: **18** | YEAR: **1996** | COUNTRY: **US** | **COLOUR** | RUNNING TIME: **104 MINUTES**

SYNOPSIS

Ex-con Corky is renovating a luxury apartment when she encounters the seductive Violet, and they soon become lovers. Together the women hatch a plot to steal a consignment of Mob money from Violet's gangster boyfriend and pin the blame on him – a scheme that is destined to go violently awry.

REVIEW

This original and intensely black comedy thriller was the entertaining directorial debut of innovative film-making brothers Larry and Andy Wachowski. It stars Jennifer Tilly and Gina Gershon as lesbian lovers who, following a series of steamy liaisons, hatch a plan to steal a fortune from the Mob and set off on a new life together. Tilly and Gershon form a convincing *Thelma and Louise*-style team, who take their punches like men, while Joe Pantoliano, as Tilly's highly strung, money laundering boyfriend, is an able foil to their conniving. Visually dynamic and strong on gallows humour, it's further proof that the Wachowski brothers' subsequent success with sci-fi action adventure *The Matrix* wasn't merely a flash in the pan. It was also a welcome career reviver for Gershon after the disastrous *Showgirls*.

LORIEN HAYNES

CAST

Jennifer Tilly *Violet* • Gina Gershon *Corky* • Joe Pantoliano *Caesar* • John P Ryan *Mickey Malnato* • Christopher Meloni *Johnny Marconi* • Richard C Sarafian *Gino Marzzone* • Barry Kivel *Shelly* • Mary Mara *Bartender*

DIRECTOR

Larry Wachowski, Andy Wachowski

SCREENPLAY

Larry Wachowski, Andy Wachowski

DVD EXTRAS

Commentary by directors and actors; cast and crew biographies; theatrical trailer; production featurette.

CONTENT ADVICE

Contains violence, swearing, sex scenes, nudity.

QUOTE UNQUOTE

I'm not apologising for what I did. I'm apologising for what I didn't do. VIOLET

IF YOU ENJOYED THIS, WHY NOT TRY ...

Les Diaboliques (1954)
The Last Seduction (1993)

DID YOU KNOW?

The Wachowskis told Joe Pantoliano to base his character on Humphrey Bogart's Fred C Dobbs in *The Treasure of the Sierra Madre*.

The Bourne Trilogy

CERTIFICATE: **12** | YEAR: **2002/2004/2007** | COUNTRY: **US/CZ REP** | **COLOUR** | RUNNING TIME: **113 MINUTES**

SYNOPSIS

Jason Bourne is rescued from the Mediterranean with bullet wounds in his back and a grave case of amnesia. When he regains consciousness, he discovers that the only clue to his identity is a laser device under his skin, which reveals the name of a Zurich bank and the numbers of a bank account.

REVIEW

The spy thriller got an exciting 21st-century makeover in a trio of hip and energetic films based on the novels by Robert Ludlum. Matt Damon stars as the amnesiac who's found floating half-dead in the Mediterranean with no means of identification, except for a device embedded in his hip containing a Swiss bank account number. Unaware that he's actually a top CIA assassin, he heads for Zurich to investigate, facing cops and government killers as his employers try to wipe out their now renegade operative. All three films are fast-paced and slickly executed, with an edgy sophistication that must have influenced the reinvention of the Bond franchise with *Casino Royale* in 2006. The final instalment directed by Paul Greengrass is particularly notable as a superbly crafted masterclass in intelligent action film-making. **SLOAN FREER/ADAM SMITH/ALAN JONES**

QUOTE UNQUOTE

Who has a safety deposit box full of money and six passports and a gun? Who has a bank account number in their hip? **JASON BOURNE**

IF YOU ENJOYED THIS, WHY NOT TRY ...
Casino Royale (2006)
The Long Kiss Goodnight (1996)

CAST

Matt Damon *Jason Bourne* • Chris Cooper *Ted Conklin* • Brian Cox *Ward Abbott* • Joan Allen *Pamela Landy* • Franka Potente *Marie Kreutz* • Julia Stiles *Nicolette "Nicky" Parsons* • David Strathairn *Noah Vosen* • Paddy Considine *Simon Ross* • Scott Glenn *Ezra Kramer* • Albert Finney *Dr Albert Hirsch* • Karl Urban *Kirill* • Clive Owen *The Professor*

DIRECTOR

Doug Liman, Paul Greengrass

SCREENPLAY

Tony Gilroy, William Blake Herron, Patrick Crowley, Paul L Sandberg, Tom Stoppard, Paul Attanasio, Scott Z Burns, George Nolfi, from the novels by Robert Ludlum

AWARDS

Academy Awards (Ultimatum) (3): Editing, Sound, Sound Editing
Baftas (Ultimatum) (2): Editing, Sound

DVD EXTRAS

The Ultimate Bourne Collection: commentaries by Doug Liman, Paul Greengrass; making-of documentaries; extended/deleted scenes; Moby music video; dvd roms with extra features; featurettes on casting, fight training, driving, roof-top stunts, special effects, music and chases; trailers. Also available on Blu-ray.

DID YOU KNOW?

Matt Damon wasn't the first actor to take on the role of Jason Bourne on screen. Richard Chamberlain played him in a 1988 *Bourne Identity* TV mini-series, which co-starred Jaclyn Smith and Denholm Elliott.

Build My Gallows High

CERTIFICATE: **PG** | YEAR: **1947** | COUNTRY: **US** | **BW** | RUNNING TIME: **92 MINUTES**

SYNOPSIS

Former private detective Jeff Bailey finds his past catching up with him when he's recognised by a customer at his gas station in the small coastal town of Bridgeport, California. The meeting reminds Bailey of the time he was hired to find the girlfriend of a gangster, who disappeared with $40,000.

REVIEW

Also known as *Out of the Past* and unfairly underrated for many years, Jacques Tourneur's film contains all the essential ingredients of the genre. There's a memorably languid performance by Robert Mitchum as the tough guy undone by his love for a gorgeous but utterly heartless *femme fatale* (played by Jane Greer), and atmospheric cinematography from the great Nicholas Musuraca. It's a stylish and highly watchable movie from French émigré Tourneur, who also made horror classics *Cat People* and *Night of the Demon*. You may have seen the 1984 remake *Against All Odds* (with Jeff Bridges and Rachel Ward), but if you want to know what *film noir* is about, this is the place to start. A line from this film, "Baby, I don't care", was used by Lee Server as the title of his 2001 Mitchum biography.

PETER FREEDMAN

CAST

Robert Mitchum *Jeff Bailey/Jeff Markham* • Jane Greer *Kathie Moffat* • Kirk Douglas *Whit Sterling* • Rhonda Fleming *Meta Carson* • Richard Webb *Jim* • Steve Brodie *Jack Fisher* • Virginia Huston *Ann Miller* • Paul Valentine *Joe Stefanos*

DIRECTOR

Jacques Tourneur

SCREENPLAY

Geoffrey Homes [Daniel Mainwaring], from his novel

DVD EXTRAS

UK DVD release as *Out of the Past*.

QUOTE UNQUOTE

You know, maybe I was wrong and luck is like love. You have to go all the way to find it. JEFF BAILEY

IF YOU ENJOYED THIS, WHY NOT TRY . . .

Against All Odds (1984)
A History of Violence (2005)

DID YOU KNOW?

The film was remade as *Against All Odds* in 1984 with Jane Greer playing the mother of her original character in *Build My Gallows High*.

Bullitt

CERTIFICATE: **15** | YEAR: **1968** | COUNTRY: **US** | **COLOUR** | RUNNING TIME: **108 MINUTES**

SYNOPSIS

San Francisco police lieutenant Frank Bullitt is assigned to protect a Mafia informant by ambitious politician Walter Chalmers, who hopes to use the case to further his career. When the witness is murdered, Bullitt covers up the crime in order to buy time to find the killers and save his job.

REVIEW

Steve McQueen did better work in his tragically shortened career, but this is one of the films that helped make him a screen icon. He's at his deadpan best as maverick cop Frank Bullitt, who's assigned to protect a key government witness against a crime syndicate. Director Peter Yates gives it more, in terms of urban reality, than the predictable script deserves, and Frank P Keller won an Oscar for editing the famous San Francisco car-bouncing hill chase between McQueen's Ford Mustang and the villains' Dodge Charger. But it's always McQueen's movie. He's snappy, laconic and cynical in equal doses, and his performance is complemented by the assured support of Robert Vaughn as sleazy politician Walter Chalmers. Only Jacqueline Bisset as Bullitt's artist girlfriend Cathy looks out of place in an underwritten role that was seemingly included as an attempt to soften the violent action.

TOM HUTCHINSON

QUOTE UNQUOTE

You work your side of the street, and I'll work mine.

FRANK BULLITT

IF YOU ENJOYED THIS, WHY NOT TRY...

Dirty Harry (1971)
The French Connection (1971)

■

CAST

Steve McQueen *Bullitt* • Robert Vaughn *Chalmers* • Jacqueline Bisset *Cathy* • Don Gordon *Delgetti* • Robert Duvall *Weissberg* • Simon Oakland *Captain Bennett* • Norman Fell *Baker* • Georg Stanford Brown *Dr Willard*

DIRECTOR

Peter Yates

SCREENPLAY

Alan R Trustman, Harry Kleiner, from the novel *Mute Witness* by Robert L Pike

AWARDS

Academy Awards (1): Editing

DVD EXTRAS

Special Edition: commentary by Peter Yates; *Steve McQueen: the Essence of Cool* documentary; *The Cutting Edge: the Magic of Movie Editing* documentary narrated by Kathy Bates; theatrical trailer. Also available on Blu-ray.

CONTENT ADVICE

Contains some violence, swearing.

DID YOU KNOW?

Having performed the famous motorcycle leap in *The Great Escape*, stunt driver Bud Ekins reteamed with Steve McQueen for the legendary car chase through the streets of San Francisco.

Cape Fear

CERTIFICATE: **15** | YEAR: **1962** | COUNTRY: **US** | **BW** | RUNNING TIME: **101 MINUTES**

SYNOPSIS

When sadistic sex offender Max Cady is released from prison, he has one plan: revenge on Sam Bowden, the respected small-town lawyer he blames for his conviction. Armed with a new-found knowledge of the law learnt during his confinement, he begins a campaign of terror against Bowden and his family.

REVIEW

Not the slick 1991 remake directed by Martin Scorsese, but the gripping and tension-laden original in which embittered ex-con Max Cady (Robert Mitchum) terrorises the family of upstanding lawyer Sam Bowden (Gregory Peck), who put him behind bars for eight years for assault. Great shocks increase the climactic suspense, with Mitchum giving a portrayal of villainy that's unforgettably vicious and sadistic. Peck is a perfect foil, his stolid decency acting as a powerful contrast to the muscular charisma of his co-star. There's also excellent support from Polly Bergen as Peck's wife, Lori Martin as his daughter and Telly Savalas as a helpful private eye. Director J Lee Thompson's skilful use of light and shadow enhances the uncomfortable mood, while the nerve-jangling score from Hitchcock regular Bernard Herrmann counterpoints the growing sense of dread with deft precision. **ALAN JONES**

CAST

Gregory Peck *Sam Bowden* • Robert Mitchum *Max Cady* • Polly Bergen *Peggy Bowden* • Lori Martin *Nancy Bowden* • Martin Balsam *Mark Dutton* • Jack Kruschen *Dave Grafton* • Telly Savalas *Charles Sievers*

DIRECTOR

J Lee Thompson

SCREENPLAY

James R Webb, from the novel *The Executioners* by John D MacDonald

DVD EXTRAS

Boxed Set: 1962 and 1991 versions of the film; making-of documentary; production photos; theatrical trailer; production notes; cast and film-makers' biographies; DVD rom; plus extras for the 1992 version.

QUOTE UNQUOTE

I got somethin' planned for your wife and kid that they ain't nevah gonna forget. They ain't nevah gonna forget it... and neither will you, counsellor! Nevah! **MAX CADY**

IF YOU ENJOYED THIS, WHY NOT TRY ...

Cape Fear (1991)
Straw Dogs (1971)

DID YOU KNOW?

During the final fight scene, Gregory Peck accidentally punched Robert Mitchum for real, prompting the bruised and battered Mitchum to comment: "I don't feel sorry for anyone dumb enough to pick a fight with him."

Capricorn One

CERTIFICATE: **PG** | YEAR: **1978** | COUNTRY: **US** | **COLOUR** | RUNNING TIME: **118 MINUTES**

SYNOPSIS

As the world watches on TV, the first manned mission to Mars touches down, while deep in the Arizona desert, three astronauts plant the US flag on a film set. Their mission is a fake, arranged to cover up a technical hitch, but when the capsule burns up on re-entry, they become a real, live problem.

REVIEW

Taking a popular conspiracy theory a stage further – did the Americans really land on the Moon, or did they fake it for a television audience in a studio? – this ingenious thriller sees three men bound for Mars, until there's a technical hitch on the launch pad. The astronauts end up faking the mission to save Nasa's face, but their space capsule (which went without them) burns up on re-entry. Problem one: three embarrassingly alive astronauts (played by James Brolin, Sam Waterston and OJ Simpson). Problem two: their distraught families. Problem three: Elliott Gould as a nosey reporter who smells a rat and starts asking awkward questions. Directed by Peter Hyams with real flair, this is hugely enjoyable, all the way to the gripping finale in which Telly Savalas relishes his fun role as an old-time crop-dusting pilot who's got the right stuff. **ADRIAN TURNER**

CAST

Elliott Gould *Robert Caulfield* • James Brolin *Charles Brubaker* • Sam Waterston *Peter Willis* • Brenda Vaccaro *Kay Brubaker* • OJ Simpson *John Walker* • Hal Holbrook *Dr James Kelloway* • Karen Black *Judy Drinkwater* • Telly Savalas *Albain*

DIRECTOR

Peter Hyams

SCREENPLAY

Peter Hyams

DVD EXTRAS

Theatrical trailers; interviews; location material. Also available on Blu-ray.

QUOTE UNQUOTE

You wouldn't know sincerity if it ran over you.
ROBERT CAULFIELD

IF YOU ENJOYED THIS, WHY NOT TRY . . .

Conspiracy Theory (1997)

■

DID YOU KNOW?

The film-makers asked Nasa for technical assistance but the request was turned down.

Chinatown

CERTIFICATE: **15** | YEAR: **1974** | COUNTRY: **US** | **COLOUR** | RUNNING TIME: **125 MINUTES**

SYNOPSIS

When private eye JJ Gittes, a former cop who specialises in divorce cases and extramarital affairs, is duped into investigating the husband of a wealthy Los Angeles socialite, he stumbles into a web of deceit and murder connected to the thirsty city's water supply. Soon Gittes is in way over his head.

REVIEW

Jack Nicholson here gives one of his best performances, playing a Los Angeles private eye called Jake Gittes, who pokes his nose rather too deeply into the lives of Faye Dunaway and her father, John Huston, a corrupt tycoon. Writer Robert Towne planned a trilogy about LA, and this first part, set in the 1930s, deals with the city's water supply and how that source of life leads to death and profit. The script – the best original work since *Citizen Kane* – is brilliantly organised, though the ending was changed when Roman Polanski arrived as director (making his first Hollywood film after the murder of his wife in 1969): Towne's story never got to Chinatown, but Polanski insisted the climax be set there. Nicholson reprised his role and also directed a belated sequel, *The Two Jakes*, but it failed to match this masterpiece, which repays any number of viewings.
ADRIAN TURNER

QUOTE UNQUOTE

See, Mr Gittes, most people never have to face the fact that, at the right time and the right place, they're capable of... anything! **NOAH CROSS**

IF YOU ENJOYED THIS, WHY NOT TRY . . .

Harper (1966)
The Two Jakes (1990)

CAST

Jack Nicholson *JJ Gittes* • Faye Dunaway *Evelyn Mulwray* • John Huston *Noah Cross* • Perry Lopez *Escobar* • John Hillerman *Yelburton* • Darrell Zwerling *Hollis Mulwray* • Diane Ladd *Ida Sessions* • Roy Jenson *Mulvihill* • Roman Polanski *Man with knife*

DIRECTOR

Roman Polanski

SCREENPLAY

Robert Towne

AWARDS

Academy Awards (1): Original Screenplay
Baftas (3): Actor (Jack Nicholson), Director, Screenplay

DVD EXTRAS

Two making-of documentaries; retrospective interview with Roman Polanaski, Jack Nicholson, Robert Towne and Robert Evans; theatrical trailer.

CONTENT ADVICE

Contains violence, swearing.

DID YOU KNOW?

Roman Polanski didn't exactly endear himself to his stars. He threw Jack Nicholson's portable TV set out of his trailer during one argument and then proceeded to pluck a stray hair from Faye Dunaway's head as it was spoiling a shot.

The Collector

CERTIFICATE: **15** | YEAR: **1965** | COUNTRY: **US/UK** | **COLOUR** | RUNNING TIME: **114 MINUTES**

SYNOPSIS

When young butterfly collector Freddie Clegg wins a large sum of money on the football pools, he buys a mansion in the country and prepares to add a human specimen to his collection – the beautiful Miranda Grey. He claims he loves her, and aims to keep her until she returns his feelings.

REVIEW

In this genuinely disturbing thriller, a maladjusted, butterfly collecting young man kidnaps an art student and keeps her in his cellar. Based on an equally disturbing and complex novel by John Fowles, this was in its day a fashionable shocker and X-certificated. Now it comes across as a fascinating period piece, featuring two quintessential 1960s stars in possibly their best roles – painfully handsome Terence Stamp as socially inept collector Freddie Clegg and beautiful, auburn-haired Samantha Eggar as the innocent victim of his attentions, Miranda Grey. Veteran William Wyler, best known for the 1939 *Wuthering Heights*, *The Best Years of Our Lives* and *Ben-Hur*, was one of the great directors of actors, and thanks to his sure handling this grim charade is both suspenseful and affecting. Wyler, Eggar and the screenplay were nominated for Oscars.

TONY SLOMAN

CAST

Terence Stamp *Freddie Clegg* • Samantha Eggar *Miranda Grey* • Mona Washbourne *Aunt Annie* • Maurice Dallimore *Neighbour* • William Beckley *Crutchley* • Gordon Barclay *Clerk*

DIRECTOR

William Wyler

SCREENPLAY

Stanley Mann, John Kohn, from the novel by John Fowles

QUOTE UNQUOTE

Don't worry. I'll respect your every privacy. **FREDDIE CLEGG**

IF YOU ENJOYED THIS, WHY NOT TRY . . .

Kiss the Girls (1997)
The Vanishing (1988)

DID YOU KNOW?

Wyler holds the record for most Oscar nominations for directing, this movie gaining his twelfth and last of them. His three wins overall put him in joint second place (with Frank Capra) behind John Ford (who has won four).

43

Coma

CERTIFICATE: **15** | YEAR: **1977** | COUNTRY: **US** | **COLOUR** | RUNNING TIME: **108 MINUTES**

SYNOPSIS

When her best friend suffers irreparable brain damage after a routine operation, Dr Susan Wheeler searches the records at Boston Memorial Hospital and uncovers an alarmingly high number of terminal coma cases, all following minor surgery. Investigating further, Dr Wheeler finds her own life in danger.

REVIEW

Geneviève Bujold's medic suspects foul play when patients start dying unexpectedly in her hospital. Presenting her findings to her boss (Richard Widmark) and the hospital's chief anaesthetist (Rip Torn), she's threatened with legal action for tampering with medical records. Even her boyfriend (Michael Douglas) has cold feet, not wishing to damage his chances of becoming chief resident. Faithfully adapted from Robin Cook's bestseller by doctor-turned-novelist Michael Crichton, this taut medical thriller has an assured sense of creepy paranoia within the absorbing central mystery that gives an extra disturbing edge to the hospital horrors. The *ER/Jurassic Park* creator also directs and expertly turns the suspense screws in the gripping way that was his trademark as the film toys with our phobias about medical institutions and surgical procedures. **ALAN JONES**

CAST

Geneviève Bujold *Dr Susan Wheeler* • Michael Douglas *Dr Mark Bellows* • Richard Widmark *Dr George A Harris* • Rip Torn *Dr George* • Elizabeth Ashley *Mrs Emerson* • Lois Chiles *Nancy Greenly* • Harry Rhodes [Hari Rhodes] *Dr Morelind* • Tom Selleck *Sean Murphy*

DIRECTOR

Michael Crichton

SCREENPLAY

Michael Crichton, from the novel by Robin Cook

CONTENT ADVICE

Contains violence, swearing, brief nudity.

QUOTE UNQUOTE

We have to do something. This is real, Mark.
DR SUSAN WHEELER

IF YOU ENJOYED THIS, WHY NOT TRY ...
Extreme Measures (1996)
Looker (1981)

DID YOU KNOW?

Michael Crichton wrote a novel with his brother, Douglas, in 1970, called *Dealing*. They combined their names for the joint authorship to make: Michael Douglas.

The Conversation

CERTIFICATE: **15** | YEAR: **1974** | COUNTRY: **US** | **COLOUR** | RUNNING TIME: **108 MINUTES**

SYNOPSIS

Harry Caul is a professional eavesdropper who's obsessed by his work and his own privacy. Following a difficult surveillance job in San Francisco, Caul is convinced a young couple are about to be murdered and gradually becomes embroiled in a mystery even more complex and dangerous than he anticipates.

REVIEW

In this small masterpiece from director Francis Ford Coppola, Gene Hackman gives a superb performance as lonely, neurotic surveillance expert Harry Caul, haunted by a past assignment in New York that left three people dead. Now based on the west coast, he's tracking the movements and voices of Frederic Forrest and Cindy Williams in San Francisco's Union Square, only to find that the marital infidelity he supposes he is observing could be part of a murder plot. Coppola tweaks the idea to surreal effect, while editor Walter Murch orchestrates the eavesdropping to produce a uniquely baffling wall of sound. Made two years after Coppola's *The Godfather*, this haunting thriller skilfully taps into post-Watergate paranoia resulting in an intensely fascinating study of a perpetrator turned victim of the surveillance society. It was nominated for three Oscars, including best sound.

TOM HUTCHINSON

QUOTE UNQUOTE

I'm not afraid of death, but I am afraid of murder.

HARRY CAUL

IF YOU ENJOYED THIS, WHY NOT TRY . . .
Blow Out (1981)
Enemy of the State (1998)

CAST

Gene Hackman *Harry Caul* • John Cazale *Stan* • Allen Garfield *"Bernie" Moran* • Frederic Forrest *Mark* • Cindy Williams *Ann* • Michael Higgins *Paul* • Elizabeth MacRae *Meredith* • Teri Garr *Amy* • Harrison Ford *Martin Stett* • Mark Wheeler *Receptionist* • Robert Shields *Mime* • Robert Duvall *The Director*

DIRECTOR

Francis Ford Coppola

SCREENPLAY

Francis Ford Coppola

AWARDS

Baftas (2): Editing, Sound

DVD EXTRAS

Commentary by Francis Ford Coppola; commentary by sound editor designer Walter Murch; *Close Up on The Conversation* featurette; theatrical trailer.

CONTENT ADVICE

Contains violence, brief nudity.

DID YOU KNOW?

Harrison Ford's role as Martin Stett was originally intended as a cameo, but his performance impressed Francis Ford Coppola and Stett became a major character in the movie.

Copycat

CERTIFICATE: **18** | YEAR: **1995** | COUNTRY: **US** | **COLOUR** | RUNNING TIME: **122 MINUTES**

SYNOPSIS

After a spate of horrific murders in the San Francisco area, homicide detective MJ Monahan seeks help from reclusive criminal psychologist Helen Hudson. As the slayings continue, Hudson believes that someone may be imitating the methods of serial killers from the past.

REVIEW

In this inventive, stylish and gripping movie, Sigourney Weaver plays a criminal psychologist who has developed chronic agoraphobia following an encounter with a serial killer (Harry Connick Jr) in a college washroom. A year later, trapped by her condition in a San Francisco apartment, she teams up with tough detective Holly Hunter to do what she can in the hunt for a multiple murderer who seems to be duplicating the crimes of his most notorious predecessors. Hunter is brilliant as the attitude-laced investigator and Weaver is equally good as the fragile, pill-popping crime victim. Add in almost unbearable suspense created by the imaginative direction of Jon Amiel (TV's *The Singing Detective*) and a super-smart script, and this mimic murder mystery is right up there with the same year's *Se7en*. **ALAN JONES**

QUOTE UNQUOTE

I'm their damn pin-up girl. They all know me. **HELEN HUDSON**

IF YOU ENJOYED THIS, WHY NOT TRY ...

The Bone Collector (1999)
The Silence of the Lambs (1991)

CAST

Sigourney Weaver *Helen Hudson* • Holly Hunter *MJ Monahan* • Dermot Mulroney *Ruben Goetz* • William McNamara *Peter Foley* • Harry Connick Jr *Daryll Lee Cullum* • Will Patton *Nicoletti* • John Rothman *Andy* • Shannon O'Hurley *Susan Schiffer*

DIRECTOR

Jon Amiel

SCREENPLAY

Ann Biderman, David Madsen

DVD EXTRAS

Commentary by Jon Amiel; production notes.

CONTENT ADVICE

Contains swearing, violence

DID YOU KNOW?

Sigourney Weaver stands a statuesque 5ft 11in, while Holly Hunter is a mere 5ft 2in. So to disguise the disparity in their height, they played many of their scenes in *Copycat* sitting down.

The Day of the Jackal

CERTIFICATE: **15** | YEAR: **1973** | COUNTRY: **UK/FR** | **COLOUR** | RUNNING TIME: **136 MINUTES**

SYNOPSIS

In 1963, having failed to murder General de Gaulle, the hardline French Secret Army Organisation decides to hire a top professional killer to do the job properly. Codenamed the "Jackal", the unassuming Englishman begins to lay his plans to assassinate one of the world's most powerful men.

REVIEW

A magnificent script from Kenneth Ross and a masterly central performance from Edward Fox form the backbone of this big-screen version of Frederick Forsyth's bestselling novel about a hired killer's mission to kill General de Gaulle. But it's Fred Zinnemann's matchless direction that makes it such compelling viewing and an object lesson in suspense as the authorities try to identify an assassin who always seems to be one step ahead of them. The pacing of the picture is superb, a methodical accumulation of detail that is as fastidious as Fox's preparation, as he closes in on his target. Although the action crisscrosses Europe, there's no postcard prettiness, just a sure grasp of the atmosphere of each place before getting down to the business of the scene. The supporting cast is also first rate, with Cyril Cusack, Michel Lonsdale and Tony Britton outstanding. **DAVID PARKINSON**

CAST
Edward Fox *The Jackal* • Michel Lonsdale *Claude Lebel* • Alan Badel *Minister* • Tony Britton *Inspector Thomas* • Adrien Cayla-Legrand *President General Charles de Gaulle* • Cyril Cusack *Gunsmith* • Donald Sinden *Mallinson* • Derek Jacobi *Caron* • Eric Porter *Colonel Rodin* • Delphine Seyrig *Colette de Montpelier* • Timothy West *Berthier*

DIRECTOR
Fred Zinnemann

SCREENPLAY
Kenneth Ross, from the novel by Frederick Forsyth

AWARDS
Baftas (1): Editing

DVD EXTRAS
Production notes; theatrical trailer.

CONTENT ADVICE
Contains violence, swearing, brief nudity.

QUOTE UNQUOTE
August 1962 was a stormy time for France...
INTRODUCTORY VOICEOVER

IF YOU ENJOYED THIS, WHY NOT TRY . . .
The Jackal (1997)
The Manchurian Candidate (1962)

DID YOU KNOW?
Michael Caine was reportedly very keen to play the Jackal, but Zinnemann thought a big star would dilute the suspense. Fox was chosen after the director enjoyed his performance in 1970's *The Go-Between*.

Dead Calm

CERTIFICATE: **15** | YEAR: **1988** | COUNTRY: **AUS** | **COLOUR** | RUNNING TIME: **96 MINUTES**

SYNOPSIS

A married couple are sailing alone on their yacht in the Pacific, taking time to come to terms with the tragic death of their young son. During the voyage, they rescue the sole survivor of a sinking schooner, a strange young man whose explanation for his predicament doesn't seem to hold water.

REVIEW

Nicole Kidman and director Phillip Noyce were catapulted into the Hollywood frontline by this scary revel, an ingenious psychological thriller in the grand Hitchcock tradition. It has a very simple premise: a couple (Kidman and Sam Neill) decide to take a yachting trip in the Pacific to try to recover from the death of their young son in a car accident. In mid-ocean, they rescue the sole survivor (Billy Zane) from a sinking schooner who claims his fellow shipmates were struck down by food poisoning. When the suspicious Neill sets out to investigate leaving Kidman to guard Zane, things take a very nasty turn indeed. As Noyce expertly cranks up the tension to fever pitch, this turns into one of the best ocean-going shockers since *Jaws*, with 21-year-old Kidman displaying the potential that would later make her one of the world's biggest stars.

ALAN JONES

CAST

Sam Neill *John Ingram* • Nicole Kidman *Rae Ingram* • Billy Zane *Hughie Warriner* • Rod Mullinar *Russell Bellows* • Joshua Tilden *Danny*

DIRECTOR

Phillip Noyce

SCREENPLAY

Terry Hayes, from the novel by Charles Williams

CONTENT ADVICE

Contains swearing, violence, nudity.

QUOTE UNQUOTE

Sorry, Rae. Whichever way I turn it, I just can't swallow it... **JOHN INGRAM**

IF YOU ENJOYED THIS, WHY NOT TRY...

Panic Room (2002)
Wait until Dark (1967)

DID YOU KNOW?

New Zealander Sam Neill came close to becoming James Bond in 1986, but was given the thumbs down by producer Albert Broccoli, who still felt let down by former Bond George Lazenby, and didn't want another antipodean in the role.

Dead Ringers

CERTIFICATE: **18** | YEAR: **1988** | COUNTRY: **CAN** | **COLOUR** | RUNNING TIME: **110 MINUTES**

SYNOPSIS

Beverly and Elliot Mantle are brilliant, identical twins who run a fertility clinic in Toronto. Psychologically, the twins are quite different, Elliot is confident whereas Beverly is shy, and when they both fall in love with the same patient, their lives take a strange and horrific turn.

REVIEW

This finely wrought urban horror tale from director David Cronenberg was inspired by the true story of identical twin gynaecologists who were found dead on New York's Upper East Side in 1975. Here, with the setting transposed to Toronto, Jeremy Irons expertly and (thanks to Cronenberg's wonderful technical skill) seamlessly plays both Beverly and Elliot Mantle, with Geneviève Bujold as the internationally famous but infertile actress who, quite literally, can't choose between them. At the time, Cronenberg was better known for more gory offerings like *Videodrome* and the 1986 remake of *The Fly*, but here he demonstrates a uniquely distressing and subtle talent, and the result is enough to put you off visiting fertility clinics for ever. Irons was reunited with Cronenberg in 1993 for his disappointing version of successful Broadway play *M Butterfly*. **TONY SLOMAN**

QUOTE UNQUOTE

I've often thought that there should be beauty contests for the *insides* of bodies. **ELLIOT MANTLE**

IF YOU ENJOYED THIS, WHY NOT TRY . . .
Raising Cain (1992)
A Zed & Two Noughts (1985)

CAST

Jeremy Irons *Beverly/Elliot Mantle* • Geneviève Bujold *Claire Niveau* • Heidi Von Palleske *Dr Cary Weiler* • Barbara Gordon *Danuta* • Shirley Douglas *Laura* • Stephen Lack *Anders Wolleck* • Nick Nichols *Leo* • Lynne Cormack *Arlene*

DIRECTOR

David Cronenberg

SCREENPLAY

David Cronenberg, Norman Snider, from the book *Twins* by Bari Wood, Jack Geasland

CONTENT ADVICE

Contains violence, swearing, a sex scene, nudity.

DID YOU KNOW?

To differentiate between the twins, Jeremy Irons located the "energy centre" of the more strident Elliot in his forehead, with the less confident Beverly's in his Adam's apple, while he put the weight on the balls or heels of his feet to suit each character.

Deliverance

CERTIFICATE: **18** | YEAR: **1972** | COUNTRY: **US** | **COLOUR** | RUNNING TIME: **104 MINUTES**

SYNOPSIS

On a weekend canoe excursion in the Appalachian mountains, four city-dwelling friends attempt to navigate a wild and uncharted river, the future of which is threatened by a dam project. But a horrific encounter with two deranged hillbillies leaves them battling both nature and man for survival.

REVIEW

Though best, if most uncomfortably, remembered for townie Ned Beatty's shocking encounter with the hillbillies in the Appalachian mountains, this provocative adult thriller from British director John Boorman is about more than shock tactics. Adapted by James Dickey from his bestselling debut novel of the same name, it charts the gradual erosion of "civilisation" by the elements, as four Atlanta businessmen on a back-to-nature canoe holiday, led by the macho Burt Reynolds, meet with disaster and destiny. It works as a piece of straightforward suspense cinema, with an uneasy atmosphere conjured from the start by the iconic "duelling banjos" scene (where Ronny Cox duets with a local musician). But it also resonates as a metaphor about masculinity under threat – and a warning not to go into the woods. **ANDREW COLLINS**

CAST

Jon Voight *Ed Gentry* • Burt Reynolds *Lewis Medlock* • Ned Beatty *Bobby Trippe* • Ronny Cox *Drew Ballinger* • Bill McKinney *Mountain man* • Herbert "Cowboy" Coward *Toothless man* • James Dickey *Sheriff Bullard*

DIRECTOR

John Boorman

SCREENPLAY

James Dickey, from his novel

DVD EXTRAS

35th Anniversary Deluxe Edition: commentary by John Boorman; featurette on the novel and its adaptation to the screen; three making-of documentaries; a look back at the impact of the film; the original behind-the-scenes documentary; theatrical trailer.

CONTENT ADVICE

Contains swearing, violence.

QUOTE UNQUOTE

Sometimes you have to lose yourself 'fore you can find anything. **LEWIS**

IF YOU ENJOYED THIS, WHY NOT TRY . . .

Southern Comfort (1981)
Wrong Turn (2003)

DID YOU KNOW?

Poet and novelist James Dickey has a cameo in the film as a sheriff.

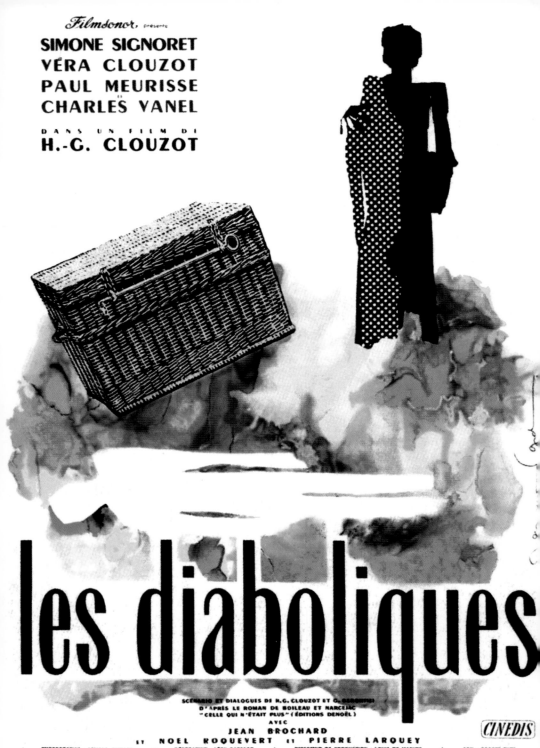

Les Diaboliques

CERTIFICATE: **15** | YEAR: **1954** | COUNTRY: **FR** | **BW** | RUNNING TIME: **112 MINUTES**

SYNOPSIS

In a provincial boys' boarding school in France, the cruelty of the headmaster drives his wife and mistress to jointly plot his death. They plan to drown him and make it appear an accident; but when the deed is done, the body disappears and the two women are only at the beginning of their nightmare.

REVIEW

In this brilliantly nasty thriller from Henri-Georges Clouzot, the wife (Vera Clouzot) and mistress (Simone Signoret) of a sadistic boarding school headmaster (Paul Meurisse) plot together to kill him – but then find his body is missing. The film's graveyard gloom is typified by the oppressive atmosphere of neglect and despair at Meurisse's school, while the final shot marvellously suggests unpleasantness to come – the climax here is one of cinema's most diabolical scenes. This is a masterpiece that easily matches the best of Hitchcock – apparently, when Clouzot bought the rights to Pierre Boileau and Thomas Narcejac's source novel *Celle Qui N'était Plus*, he was nearly beaten to it by the Master of Suspense who was only a couple of hours behind him.

TOM HUTCHINSON

CAST

Simone Signoret *Nicole Horner* • Vera Clouzot *Christina Delassalle* • Paul Meurisse *Michel Delassalle* • Charles Vanel *Inspector Fichet* • Pierre Larquey *M Drain* • Noël Roquevert *M Herboux* • Jean Brochard *Plantiveau* • Thérèse Dorny *Mme Herboux* • Michel Serrault *Raymond*

DIRECTOR

Henri-Georges Clouzot

SCREENPLAY

Henri-Georges Clouzot, Jérôme Géromini, Frédéric Grendel, René Masson, from the novel *Celle Qui N'Etait Plus* by Pierre Boileau, Thomas Narcejac

DVD EXTRAS

Two versions: one has stills gallery; poster gallery; cast and crew biographies; theatrical trailer; and theatrical trailer for *Wages of Fear*. Another version exists with a commentary by Susan Hayward, an expert on French cinema who has written a book about the film and another on Simone Signoret.

QUOTE UNQUOTE

There is something going on here that can only accurately be described as mysterious – very mysterious indeed!

NICOLE HORNER

IF YOU ENJOYED THIS, WHY NOT TRY . . .

Bound (1996)
Fear in the Night (1947)

DID YOU KNOW?

American film critic Roger Ebert reckons the dishevelled, cigar-chomping Inspector Fichet in this movie inspired Peter Falk's characterisation of Columbo.

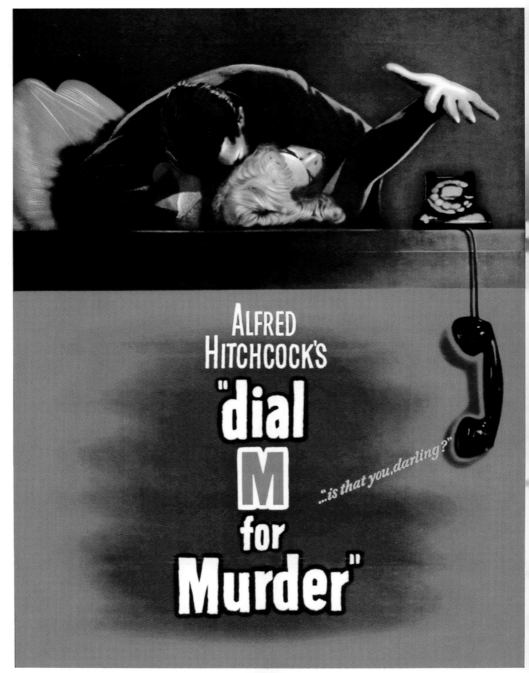

ALFRED
HITCHCOCK'S

"dial
M
for
Murder"

"...is that you, darling?"

PRESENTED BY WARNER BROS.

RAY MILLAND · GRACE KELLY · ROBERT CUMMINGS   WARNERCOLOR

WITH JOHN WILLIAMS DIRECTED BY ALFRED HITCHCOCK WRITTEN BY FREDERICK KNOTT who wrote the International Stage Success

Dial M for Murder

CERTIFICATE: **PG** | YEAR: **1954** | COUNTRY: **US** | **COLOUR** | RUNNING TIME: **100 MINUTES**

SYNOPSIS

When he discovers that his wealthy wife Margot is having an affair with novelist Mark Halliday, retired tennis player Tony Wendice hatches a plot to have her killed by an "intruder", ensuring he'll be able to sustain his playboy lifestyle. But the best-laid plans of homicidal husbands...

REVIEW

Alfred Hitchcock only took on this version of Frederick Knott's play to fulfil his Warners contract. Such was his lack of interest in the project that he claimed he could have phoned in his direction and that the action wouldn't have been any less interesting if he had staged it in a phone box. It's true to say that many of the set pieces literally fall flat, because they were originally composed for presentation in 3-D, but as Ray Milland plots to bump off wife Grace Kelly there are plenty of deft touches that loudly proclaim "genius at work". Milland's sinister sophistication catches the eye, but it's Kelly's subtly shaded suffering that really stands out. In the first of three consecutive collaborations with the Master of Suspense, she's superb as the spouse whose deepening affection for mystery writer Robert Cummings puts her life in danger. **DAVID PARKINSON**

CAST

Ray Milland *Tony Wendice* • Grace Kelly *Margot Wendice* • Robert Cummings *Mark Halliday* • John Williams *Chief Inspector Hubbard* • Anthony Dawson *Captain Lesgate* • Patrick Allen *Pearson* • George Leigh *William* • George Alderson *Detective* • Robin Hughes *Police sergeant*

DIRECTOR

Alfred Hitchcock

SCREENPLAY

Frederick Knott, from his play

QUOTE UNQUOTE

Do you really believe in the perfect murder? **MARGOT WENDICE**

IF YOU ENJOYED THIS, WHY NOT TRY . . .

Suspicion (1941)
What Lies Beneath (2000)

■

DID YOU KNOW?

As Grace Kelly's plight deepens, her costumes are made from increasingly darker and drabber materials.

Dirty Harry

CERTIFICATE: **18** | YEAR: **1971** | COUNTRY: **US** | **COLOUR** | RUNNING TIME: **102 MINUTES**

SYNOPSIS

San Francisco cop "Dirty" Harry Callahan is assigned the case of a sniper who has murdered a young girl and threatened further killings if his ransom demand is not met. Dismayed at being partnered with a raw recruit, Callahan is also at odds with his bosses over dancing to a killer's tune.

REVIEW

Movie history might have run differently had Frank Sinatra not injured his hand, causing him to relinquish the role of renegade cop "Dirty" Harry Callahan to Clint Eastwood. This is the first and best outing for Eastwood's San Francisco police inspector, in which he tramples on the American Constitution to bring gibbering psycho Andrew Robinson to justice. (Robinson's "Scorpio" character is based on the notorious real-life killer whose crimes were the subject of *Zodiac*.) Directed by Don Siegel with his usual toughness and crisp efficiency, this is a masterpiece of action movie-making. Eastwood displays all the hard-boiled traits that are now part of his screen persona and cinema folklore. Making good use of Golden Gate locations, and armed with a smart and darkly cynical script, this original generates an excitement that none of the four sequels could match. **ALAN JONES**

QUOTE UNQUOTE

I know what you're thinking: "Did he fire six shots or only five?" **HARRY CALLAHAN**

IF YOU ENJOYED THIS, WHY NOT TRY ...

Magnum Force (1973)
Shaft (1971)

CAST

Clint Eastwood *Harry Callahan* • Harry Guardino *Lieutenant Bressler* • Reni Santoni *Chico* • John Vernon *Mayor* • Andy Robinson [Andrew Robinson] *Killer* • John Larch *Chief* • John Mitchum *DeGeorgio* • Mae Mercer *Mrs Russell*

DIRECTOR

Don Siegel

SCREENPLAY

Harry Julian Fink, Rita M Fink, Dean Riesner, from a story by Harry Julian Fink, Rita M Fink

DVD EXTRAS

Two-disc Special Edition: commentary by Richard Schickel; interview gallery; *Dirty Harry's Way* featurette; trailers; *The Long Shadow of Dirty Harry* featurette; *Clint Eastwood: The Man from Malpaso* 1993 TV special. Also available on Blu-ray.

CONTENT ADVICE

Contains violence, swearing, brief nudity.

DID YOU KNOW?

Carry On regular Kenneth Williams was one of the film's biggest fans.

Don't Look Now

CERTIFICATE: **15** | YEAR: **1973** | COUNTRY: **UK/IT** | **COLOUR** | RUNNING TIME: **105 MINUTES**

SYNOPSIS

Following the tragic drowning of their young daughter, John and Laura Baxter go to Venice – he to work, she to recuperate. There they meet a woman who claims to be able to communicate with the dead child. Caught up in the bizarre events that follow, the Baxters are drawn towards a forbidding fate.

REVIEW

Perhaps best known for the fiercely erotic scene of love-making between Donald Sutherland and Julie Christie which forms the sensual core of this supernatural chiller, director Nicolas Roeg's masterpiece has much more to it than notoriety. Adapted from a Daphne du Maurier short story, this superbly atmospheric tale offers a time-distorted vision of terror set in wintertime Venice, portrayed here as a hostile city of brooding silences and fog-shrouded canals. Church restorer Sutherland and wife Christie are there after the death of their young daughter, and it is in the City of Water that the spectral presence of their child draws them into a labyrinth of cryptic signs and doom-laden portents. Hilary Mason and Clelia Matania add intrigue as the sisters who pique the couple's interest, and the fear-drenched mood of alienation is sustained right up until the unforgettable climax. **TOM HUTCHINSON**

CAST

Donald Sutherland *John Baxter* • Julie Christie *Laura Baxter* • Hilary Mason *Heather* • Clelia Matania *Wendy* • Massimo Serato *Bishop Barbarrigo* • Renato Scarpa *Inspector Longhi* • David Tree *Anthony Babbage*

DIRECTOR

Nicolas Roeg

SCREENPLAY

Allan Scott, Chris Bryant, from a short story by Daphne du Maurier

AWARDS

Baftas (1): Cinematography

DVD EXTRAS

Special Edition: introduction from Alan Jones; commentary by Nicolas Roeg; *Looking Back* – a making-of documentary including interviews with Roeg, the cinematographer and editor; interview with composer Pino Donnagio; booklet including behind-the-scenes stills and an essay by 1970s cinema expert Ryan Gilbey.

CONTENT ADVICE

Contains violence, swearing, nudity.

QUOTE UNQUOTE

This one who's blind. She's the one that can see.
LAURA BAXTER

IF YOU ENJOYED THIS, WHY NOT TRY ...
Antichrist (2009)

■

DID YOU KNOW?

Donald Sutherland named his son Roeg after this film's director.

Double Indemnity

CERTIFICATE: **PG** | YEAR: **1944** | COUNTRY: **US** | **BW** | RUNNING TIME: **103 MINUTES**

SYNOPSIS

Insurance salesman Walter Neff is seduced by Phyllis Dietrichson into killing her wealthy husband and making his death seem like an accident so they can claim his life insurance using a double indemnity clause. But Neff's best friend and boss, insurance analyst Barton Keyes, suspects foul play.

REVIEW

This classic thriller from director Billy Wilder is one of the best-loved examples of *film noir* ever made. Based on a short story by James M Cain (author of *The Postman Always Rings Twice*), and with a crackling screenplay co-written by Raymond Chandler, it follows definitive *femme fatale* Barbara Stanwyck as she seduces insurance salesman Fred MacMurray into doing away with her husband to claim his life insurance. But dogged claims investigator Edward G Robinson smells a rat. Wilder keeps the sexual tension tight and displays a mastery of visualisation on key plot points. Some may find Stanwyck less sexy than her character should be, but that's a minor quibble. Wilder was nominated for an Oscar, as was John F Seitz's cinematography and Miklos Rozsa's score. In the best actress category, Stanwyck lost out to Ingrid Bergman for *Gaslight*.

TONY SLOMAN

QUOTE UNQUOTE

I killed him for money – and a woman – and I didn't get the money and I didn't get the woman. **WALTER NEFF**

IF YOU ENJOYED THIS, WHY NOT TRY ...

The Postman Always Rings Twice (1946)
Romeo Is Bleeding (1992)

CAST

Fred MacMurray *Walter Neff* • Barbara Stanwyck *Phyllis Dietrichson* • Edward G Robinson *Barton Keyes* • Porter Hall *Mr Jackson* • Jean Heather *Lola Dietrichson* • Tom Powers *Mr Dietrichson* • Byron Barr *Nino Zachette*

DIRECTOR

Billy Wilder

SCREENPLAY

Billy Wilder, Raymond Chandler, from the novella by James M Cain, as serialised in *Liberty* magazine

DID YOU KNOW?

In the original screenplay, the insurance salesman is called Walter Ness. However, just before shooting began, a real-life insurance salesman of that name was found to be living in Beverly Hills, so he became Walter Neff. In the novel, he's Walter Huff.

Dressed to Kill

CERTIFICATE: **18** | YEAR: **1980** | COUNTRY: **US** | **COLOUR** | RUNNING TIME: **100 MINUTES**

SYNOPSIS

Despite the attentions of psychiatrist Dr Robert Elliott, frustrated housewife Kate Miller remains unhappy until an encounter at a museum offers her the opportunity to fulfil her romantic fantasies. But she awakens from the ensuing liaison to face a series of unpleasant and horrifying surprises.

REVIEW

Brian De Palma does his witty Hitchcock imitation again, but here adds his own trademark layers of macabre black comedy and visual ingenuity to the *Psycho*-influenced proceedings. When sex-starved, 40-something housewife Angie Dickinson attempts to inject a little excitement into her mundane life, she becomes involved in a lethal situation, into which her techno-geek son Keith Gordon and prostitute Nancy Allen (then the director's wife) are swiftly dragged. An eyebrow-raising performance from Michael Caine as a psychiatrist and the presence of Dennis Franz (*Hill Street Blues*) as a detective keep this clever shocker moving along nicely, while De Palma's brilliant sleight-of-hand direction (the museum sequence is a stand out) pulls out all the suspense stops and provides some unforgettable jolts. Pino Donaggio's marvellous score is a major plus, too. **ALAN JONES**

CAST

Michael Caine *Dr Robert Elliott* • Angie Dickinson *Kate Miller* • Nancy Allen *Liz Blake* • Keith Gordon *Peter Miller* • Dennis Franz *Detective Marino* • David Margulies *Dr Levy*

DIRECTOR

Brian De Palma

SCREENPLAY

Brian De Palma

DVD EXTRAS

Theatrical trailer.

CONTENT ADVICE

Contains swearing, violence, sex scenes, nudity.

QUOTE UNQUOTE

Oh, I borrowed your razor... and, well, you'll read all about it. **VOICE OF BOBBI**

IF YOU ENJOYED THIS, WHY NOT TRY . . .

No Way to Treat a Lady (1968)
Psycho (1960)

DID YOU KNOW?

Brian De Palma found inspiration in a sequence in Gerald Walker's novel *Cruising* in which a serial killer of gay men selects a female victim in a museum to put the cops off the trail. This idea became the basis of this Hitchcock homage.

The most bizarre murder weapon ever used!

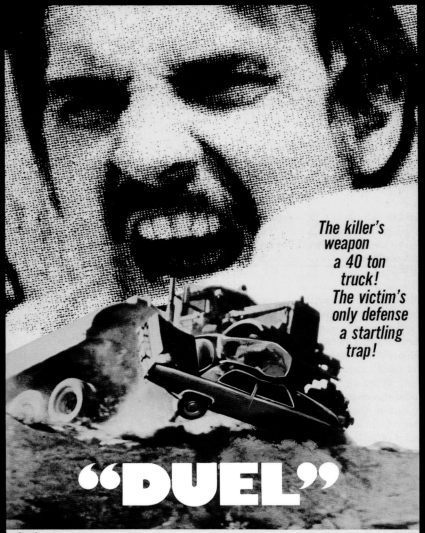

The killer's weapon a 40 ton truck! The victim's only defense a startling trap!

"DUEL"

Starring
DENNIS WEAVER Screenplay by RICHARD MATHESON • Based on his published story
Directed by STEVEN SPIELBERG • Produced by GEORGE ECKSTEIN • A UNIVERSAL PICTURE TECHNICOLOR®
Distributed by Cinema International Corporation

Duel

CERTIFICATE: **PG** | YEAR: **1972** | COUNTRY: **US** | **COLOUR** | RUNNING TIME: **85 MINUTES**

SYNOPSIS

On an isolated stretch of desert road in California, a harried businessman with a deadline overtakes a tanker truck. This sparks a deadly game of cat-and-mouse as the hapless commuter is stalked by his smoke-spewing nemesis whose sole purpose seems to be to crush him under its gigantic wheels.

REVIEW

Made for US television by the 20-something Steven Spielberg, this thriller proved such a hit that it enjoyed a theatrical release in Europe and launched the young director's career in movies. The pitch is simplicity itself: businessman Dennis Weaver in his red Plymouth Valiant is terrorised by an anonymously driven truck on a stretch of Californian desert highway. Shot on location in 13 days for next to nothing, there's barely any dialogue – it's all palm-moistening, tyre-squealing action – but once you've seen it, you'll never forget it. Adapted by *I Am Legend* author Richard Matheson from his own short story, it works as a parable about urban paranoia or as a rollercoaster thriller that never lets up. The truck itself prefigures Spielberg's shark in *Jaws* as a marauding screen monster with a personality of its own.
ANDREW COLLINS

CAST

Dennis Weaver *David Mann* • Jacqueline Scott *Mrs Mann* • Eddie Firestone *Cafe owner* • Lou Frizzell *Bus driver* • Gene Dynarski *Man in cafe* • Lucille Benson *Lady at Snakarama*

DIRECTOR

Steven Spielberg

SCREENPLAY

Richard Matheson, from his story

DVD EXTRAS

Special Edition: making-of featurette with Steven Spielberg; *Steven Spielberg and the Small Screen* featurette; Richard Matheson on the script; photo gallery; cast and crew biographies; production notes; theatrical trailer.

QUOTE UNQUOTE

I'd like to report a truck driver who's been endangering my life. **DAVID MANN**

IF YOU ENJOYED THIS, WHY NOT TRY . . .

Jaws (1975)
Road Kill (2001)

DID YOU KNOW?

On the day that President Kennedy was assassinated (22 November 1963), a truck came too close to author Richard Matheson's car and the story of *Duel* was born.

11:20:98

A
DON SIMPSON/JERRY BRUCKHEIMER
PRODUCTION

A FILM BY
TONY SCOTT

WILL SMITH   GENE HACKMAN

ENEMY OF THE STATE

IT'S NOT
PARANOIA
IF THEY'RE REALLY
AFTER YOU.

11:20:98

WILL SMITH   GENE HACKMAN

ENEMY OF THE STATE

TOUCHSTONE PICTURES PRESENTS
A DON SIMPSON/JERRY BRUCKHEIMER PRODUCTION
IN ASSOCIATION WITH SCOTT FREE PRODUCTIONS A FILM BY TONY SCOTT WILL SMITH
GENE HACKMAN "ENEMY OF THE STATE" JON VOIGHT
REGINA KING LOREN DEAN JAKE BUSEY BARRY PEPPER
AND GABRIEL BYRNE MUSIC BY TREVOR RABIN AND HARRY GREGSON-WILLIAMS
COSTUME DESIGNER MARLENE STEWART FILM EDITOR CHRIS LEBENZON
PRODUCTION DESIGNER BENJAMIN FERNANDEZ DIRECTOR OF PHOTOGRAPHY DAN MINDEL
EXECUTIVE PRODUCERS CHAD OMAN AND JAMES W. SKOTCHDOPOLE
AND ANDREW Z. DAVIS WRITTEN BY DAVID MARCONI AND AARON SORKIN
AND HENRY BEAN & TONY GILROY PRODUCED BY JERRY BRUCKHEIMER
DIRECTED BY TONY SCOTT

Enemy of the State

CERTIFICATE: **15** | YEAR: **1998** | COUNTRY: **US** | **COLOUR** | RUNNING TIME: **133 MINUTES**

SYNOPSIS

Successful lawyer Robert Clayton Dean is out shopping when evidence of a political assassination is slipped into his possession. Soon the bewildered Dean is on the run, trying to stay one step ahead of a sinister adversary who has an arsenal of hi-tech gadgetry at his disposal.

REVIEW

In this intriguing and scarily thought-provoking movie, Will Smith gives a winning central performance as Washington DC lawyer Robert Clayton Dean, whose life is ruined when an incriminating tape revealing the murder of a congressman (Jason Robards) accidentally ends up in his possession. Relentlessly pursued by a corrupt government official (Jon Voight) and his posse of electronic trackers, who use spy satellites, transmitters and all manner of undercover gizmos to trace him, Dean fights a desperate battle to clear his name. Expert direction by Tony Scott gives the cracking, frenetically paced events extra edge and appeal, and there's a nod to Francis Ford Coppola's 1974 psychological thriller *The Conversation* in the casting of Gene Hackman as a former spy who informs Dean of the ins and outs of the surveillance game. **ALAN JONES**

CAST

Will Smith *Robert Clayton Dean* • Gene Hackman *Brill* • Jon Voight *Reynolds* • Lisa Bonet *Rachel Banks* • Regina King *Carla Dean* • Ian Hart *Bingham* • Jason Lee *Zavitz* • Gabriel Byrne *"Brill"* • Jason Robards *Hammersly* • Tom Sizemore *Pintero*

DIRECTOR

Tony Scott

SCREENPLAY

David Marconi

DVD EXTRAS

Special Edition: deleted scenes; behind-the-scenes featurette; making-of documentary. There is also a version with an extended cut of the film, but no other extras. Also available on Blu-ray.

CONTENT ADVICE

Contains swearing, violence.

QUOTE UNQUOTE

If you live another day, I'll be very impressed. BRILL

IF YOU ENJOYED THIS, WHY NOT TRY . . .

Body of Lies (2008)
The Conversation (1974)

DID YOU KNOW?

In 1958, acting students at the Pasadena Playhouse voted classmate Gene Hackman "Least Likely to Succeed" along with another young hopeful. His partner in shame? Dustin Hoffman. Both are now two-time Oscar winners.

Falling Down

CERTIFICATE: **18** | YEAR: **1992** | COUNTRY: **US/FR** | **COLOUR** | RUNNING TIME: **107 MINUTES**

SYNOPSIS

When William Foster finds himself in gridlock during the Los Angeles rush hour, the heat of the day and the frustration of his empty life finally make him snap. He abandons his car, determined to "go home" to his ex-wife and daughter – a journey during which the violent mayhem just keeps escalating.

REVIEW

Made from a script that was rejected by every major Hollywood studio, this is a storming portrait of urban alienation in America. Some stateside critics were quick to brand the film racist, as Michael Douglas's white-collar worker snaps one day, abandons his car in gridlock and engages in a violent spree that sees him destroy a Korean store and take on a Latino gang. But Douglas is no racist vigilante. In director Joel Schumacher's bold, believable and darkly funny film, he is a man consumed by rage at his own powerlessness, who reacts with violence to anyone who tries to prevent him from reaching "home" – now more of a concept than a place. The film loses momentum towards the end, but Douglas gives a superb performance and he's matched by the excellent Robert Duvall as an ageing, world-weary cop tackling his last case before retirement.
DAVID PARKINSON

CAST

Michael Douglas *D-Fens, William Foster* • Robert Duvall *Prendergast* • Barbara Hershey *Beth* • Rachel Ticotin *Sandra* • Tuesday Weld *Mrs Prendergast* • Frederic Forrest *Surplus Store owner* • Lois Smith *D-Fens's mother* • Joey Hope Singer *Adele*

DIRECTOR

Joel Schumacher

SCREENPLAY

Ebbe Roe Smith

DVD EXTRAS

Theatrical trailer. Also available on Blu-ray.

CONTENT ADVICE

Contains swearing, violence.

QUOTE UNQUOTE

You have a choice. I can kill you. Or you can kill me, and my daughter will get the insurance. **WILLIAM FOSTER**

IF YOU ENJOYED THIS, WHY NOT TRY...

Network (1976)

DID YOU KNOW?

The 1992 Los Angeles riots broke out as *Falling Down* was being filmed.

Farewell My Lovely

CERTIFICATE: **PG** | YEAR: **1944** | COUNTRY: **US** | **BW** | RUNNING TIME: **91 MINUTES**

SYNOPSIS

Blindfolded and under suspicion of murder, private eye Philip Marlowe recalls the events that followed when he was hired to find a woman called Velma, the former girlfriend of ex-convict Moose Malloy. The case soon bleeds into another – the theft of a necklace – with double-crosses all around.

REVIEW

Also known by its American title *Murder, My Sweet*, this terrific adaptation of the Raymond Chandler novel was the movie that established former crooner Dick Powell's new hard-boiled image. He out-Bogies Bogart playing the impoverished private eye Philip Marlowe, caught up in two tough and nasty cases that eventually dovetail into one. Quintessential *film noir*, this is superbly directed by Edward Dmytryk, with an economic use of voiceover that now stands as a skilful example of the device. Mike Mazurki is a perfect Moose Malloy, but it's Claire Trevor as Velma that you'll remember. Parts of the plot were used previously in *The Falcon Takes Over*, and the film was later remade with Robert Mitchum as Marlowe, but this tight black-and-white masterpiece is as good as it gets. **TONY SLOMAN**

QUOTE UNQUOTE

My throat felt sore, but the fingers feeling it didn't feel anything. They were just a bunch of bananas that looked like fingers. **PHILIP MARLOWE**

IF YOU ENJOYED THIS, WHY NOT TRY . . .
The Big Sleep (1946)
Farewell, My Lovely (1975)

CAST

Dick Powell *Philip Marlowe* • Claire Trevor *Mrs Grayle/Velma Valento* • Anne Shirley *Ann Grayle* • Otto Kruger *Jules Amthor* • Mike Mazurki *Moose Malloy* • Miles Mander *Mr Grayle* • Douglas Walton *Lindsay Marriott*

DIRECTOR
Edward Dmytryk

SCREENPLAY
John Paxton, from the novel by Raymond Chandler

DID YOU KNOW?
Raymond Chandler praised Dick Powell's portrayal of Philip Marlowe, though director Edward Dmytryk was initially appalled that the ageing matinee idol had been cast.

Fargo

CERTIFICATE: **18** | YEAR: **1995** | COUNTRY: **US** | **COLOUR** | RUNNING TIME: **94 MINUTES**

SYNOPSIS

Car salesman Jerry Lundegaard arranges to have his wife kidnapped in order to extort money from his wealthy father-in-law. But thanks to a spectacularly inept pair of criminals, his scheme fails to go as planned and heavily pregnant local police chief Marge Gunderson is soon on the bloody case.

REVIEW

The Coen brothers (director/writer Joel, producer/writer Ethan) are on top form with this quirky, unconventional, comedy-tinged crime thriller set in snowy Minnesota. Amateur kidnappers Steve Buscemi and Peter Stormare leave a trail of dead bodies that is investigated, with rare instinct and understanding, by heavily pregnant police chief Frances McDormand (who won an Oscar for her performance). Supposedly inspired by a true story, the Coens neatly subvert thriller clichés for their own surreal and philosophical ends, while retaining the genre's old-fashioned virtues and screw-tightening tension. Sweet-natured mirth is combined with deliciously twisted malice, and gory horror merges with offbeat humour, while the whole is set against an extraordinary winter wonderland backdrop. The result is a modern masterpiece. **ALAN JONES**

QUOTE UNQUOTE

I'm not sure I agree with you a hundred per cent on your police work, there, Lou. **MARGE GUNDERSON**

IF YOU ENJOYED THIS, WHY NOT TRY . . .
Death in Brunswick (1990)
A Simple Plan (1998)

CAST

Frances McDormand *Marge Gunderson* • William H Macy *Jerry Lundegaard* • Steve Buscemi *Carl Showalter* • Peter Stormare *Gaear Grimsrud* • Harve Presnell *Wade Gustafson* • Kristin Rudrud *Jean Lundegaard* • Tony Denman *Scotty Lundegaard* • Kurt Schweickhardt *Car salesman*

DIRECTOR

Joel Coen

SCREENPLAY

Ethan Coen, Joel Coen

AWARDS

Academy Awards (2): Actress (Frances McDormand), Original Screenplay
Baftas (1): Director

DVD EXTRAS

Special Edition: *Minnesota Nice* an insight into the peculiarities of the region; interview with the Coen brothers; commentary by producers Tim Bevan and Eric Fellner; commentary by director of photography Roger Deakins; *The Coen Brothers Repertory Company* interactive guide; photo gallery; trivia tracks; *American Cinematographer* article; theatrical trailers; TV spots. Also available on Blu-ray.

DID YOU KNOW?

Norm Gunderson's competition for the duck stamps are the real-life Hautman brothers, Jim, Robert and Joe, who frequently win wildlife stamp competitions. They have been close friends of the Coens since childhood and are thanked on the movie credits.

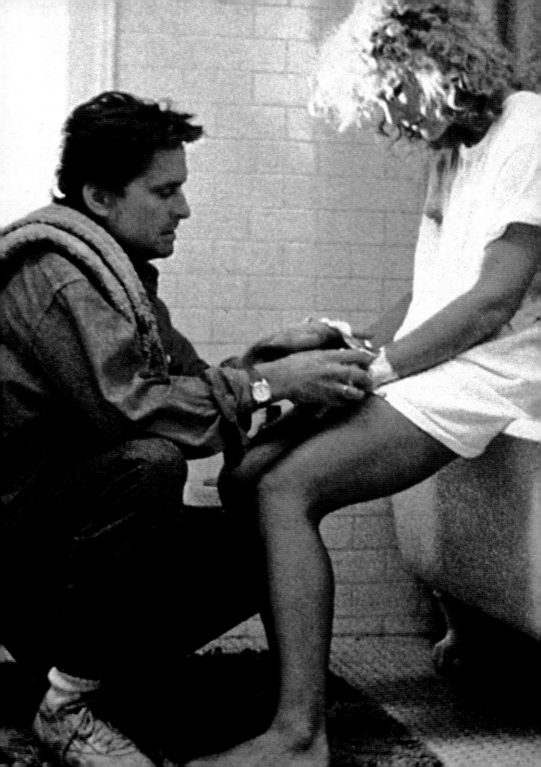

Fatal Attraction

CERTIFICATE: **18** | YEAR: **1987** | COUNTRY: **US** | **COLOUR** | RUNNING TIME: **114 MINUTES**

SYNOPSIS

While his wife and daughter are away, Manhattan lawyer Dan Gallagher has a passionate fling with Alex Forrest, an unmarried woman he meets at a party. Gallagher sees it as a one-night stand, but Forrest finds his rejection hard to accept and begins an increasingly desperate campaign to win him back.

REVIEW

This is the movie that, among other things, helped create a new genre: the crazed female from hell (see *Basic Instinct*, *The Hand That Rocks the Cradle* and *The Crush* for prime examples). Glenn Close plays the obsessed woman driven to extreme lengths when she discovers that Michael Douglas is not going to leave his wife (Anne Archer) for her. Close is excellent in a thankless role, while Douglas established himself as the troubled icon of middle-class America, the ordinary man who would later find himself getting out of his depth in the likes of *Falling Down* and *Disclosure*. The movie's message (it's all right to have an affair as long as it's not with a nutcase) is more than a little dubious, but there's no denying its slick power, and director Adrian Lyne milks the tension for all it's worth. JOHN FERGUSON

CAST

Michael Douglas *Dan Gallagher* • Glenn Close *Alex Forrest* • Anne Archer *Beth Gallagher* • Ellen Hamilton Latzen *Ellen Gallagher* • Stuart Pankin *Jimmy* • Ellen Foley *Hildy* • Fred Gwynne *Arthur* • Meg Mundy *Joan Rogerson*

DIRECTOR

Adrian Lyne

SCREENPLAY

James Dearden

AWARDS

Baftas (1): Editing

DVD EXTRAS

Special Collector's Edition: commentary by Adrian Lyne; alternative ending with director's introduction; *Forever Fatal: Remembering Fatal Attraction* featurette; *Social Attraction: a Look at the Cultural Phenomenon of Fatal Attraction*; behind-the-scenes featurette; rehearsal footage; theatrical trailer.

CONTENT ADVICE

Contains violence, swearing, sex scenes, nudity.

QUOTE UNQUOTE

Well, what am I supposed to do? You won't answer my calls, you change your number. I mean, I'm not gonna be ignored, Dan! ALEX FORREST

IF YOU ENJOYED THIS, WHY NOT TRY . . .

Basic Instinct (1992)
Disclosure (1994)

DID YOU KNOW?

Glenn Close took the knife she used in the movie as a souvenir and hung it in her kitchen.

ALFRED HITCHCOCK'S FRENZY

JON FINCH · ALEC McCOWEN · BARRY FOSTER
BILLIE WHITELAW · ANNA MASSEY · BARBARA LEIGH-HUNT · BERNARD CRIBBINS · VIVIEN MERCHANT
ANTHONY SHAFFER **ALFRED HITCHCOCK**
UNIVERSAL FILM IN TECHNICOLOR® CINEMA INTERNATIONAL CORPORATION

Frenzy

CERTIFICATE: **18** | YEAR: **1972** | COUNTRY: **UK** | **COLOUR** | RUNNING TIME: **111 MINUTES**

SYNOPSIS

London is being terrorised by a series of brutal "necktie murders" and a naked female body found in the Thames is confirmed as the latest victim. Suspicion falls on an ex-RAF officer, and a personal tragedy soon makes his guilt seem certain. Can he clear his name before the police close in?

REVIEW

Alfred Hitchcock's penultimate film saw him return to his British roots with this thriller about a "necktie" murderer at large in London. Jon Finch plays the chief suspect but, as usual, Hitchcock is more interested in black humour and clever camerawork than a simple whodunnit. Lots of typical Hitchcockian touches are on show (the wrong man theme; fleeing footsteps at the edge of our view; a shocking corpse when least expected). The gratuitous violence and nudity are not so typical (it was the first Hitchcock film to feature nudity), while the director seems to show mysogynistic tendencies more obviously here than in his earlier movies. *Sleuth* author Anthony Shaffer wrote the screenplay, and there's plenty of other British talent on display, including Alec McCowen, Vivien Merchant and the excellent Billie Whitelaw. It's not the very best Hitchcock, but it remains a truly unsettling piece.

SUE HEAL

CAST

Jon Finch *Richard Blaney* • Alec McCowen *Chief Inspector Oxford* • Barry Foster *Robert Rusk* • Barbara Leigh-Hunt *Brenda Blaney* • Anna Massey *Babs Milligan* • Vivien Merchant *Mrs Oxford* • Bernard Cribbins *Felix Forsythe* • Billie Whitelaw *Hetty Porter* • Rita Webb *Mrs Rusk* • Jean Marsh *Monica Barley*

DIRECTOR

Alfred Hitchcock

SCREENPLAY

Anthony Shaffer, from the novel *Goodbye Piccadilly, Farewell Leicester Square* by Arthur LaBern

DVD EXTRAS

Making-of documentary; art gallery; theatrical trailer.

CONTENT ADVICE

Contains violence, swearing.

QUOTE UNQUOTE

Mr Rusk, you're not wearing your tie. CHIEF INSPECTOR OXFORD

IF YOU ENJOYED THIS, WHY NOT TRY . . .

The Boston Strangler (1968)
The Wrong Man (1956)

■

DID YOU KNOW?

In keeping with the macabre tone of *Frenzy*, the trailers featured a dummy cadaver of director Alfred Hitchcock, seen floating down the Thames. In the film (the first by Hitch with nudity), the body was that of the "necktie murderer's" most recent victim.

Get Carter

CERTIFICATE: **18** | YEAR: **1971** | COUNTRY: **UK** | **COLOUR** | RUNNING TIME: **106 MINUTES**

SYNOPSIS

London gangster Jack Carter travels to the north east of England to shed light on the mysterious death of his brother. He uncovers a conspiracy involving his teenage niece, blue movies, local villains and certain "respectable" citizens. When he learns enough, he plans his revenge.

REVIEW

This terrific, tough British thriller hides its story of raw revenge behind some fascinating Newcastle upon Tyne locations, courtesy of cinematographer Wolfgang Suschitzky, and its impact remains undiminished. Director Mike Hodges keeps a firm hand on the surly proceedings and Michael Caine is at his most impressively impassive as London gangster Jack Carter, who goes north after his brother is murdered and finds his teenage niece involved in a blue-film racket. His investigations lead him to North East crime boss Cyril Kinnear, who's portrayed with a razor-slash presence by playwright John Osborne. Hodges may tip his hat to Raymond Chandler and hard-boiled American crime fiction by having Caine read *Farewell, My Lovely* on the train to Newcastle, but his movie is sex and death with a British accent and a welcome change from the more familiar American-set thrillers of today. **TOM HUTCHINSON**

CAST
Michael Caine *Jack Carter* • John Osborne *Cyril Kinnear* • Ian Hendry *Eric Paice* • Britt Ekland *Anna Fletcher* • Bryan Mosley *Cliff Brumby* • Geraldine Moffat *Glenda* • Dorothy White *Margaret* • Alun Armstrong *Keith*

DIRECTOR
Mike Hodges

SCREENPLAY
Mike Hodges, from the novel *Jack's Return Home* by Ted Lewis

DVD EXTRAS
Commentary by Mike Hodges, Michael Caine and cinematographer Wolfgang Suzitchsky; three theatrical trailers; Roy Budd plays the theme tune; Michael Caine trailer; isolated music track; cast & crew information.

QUOTE UNQUOTE
You're a big man, but you're in bad shape. With me it's a full-time job. **JACK CARTER**

IF YOU ENJOYED THIS, WHY NOT TRY . . .
Point Blank (1967)

DID YOU KNOW?
Producer Michael Klinger allowed his own white Cadillac to be used in this 1971 thriller.

The Getaway

CERTIFICATE: **18** | YEAR: **1972** | COUNTRY: **US** | **COLOUR** | RUNNING TIME: **117 MINUTES**

SYNOPSIS

A wealthy businessman arranges early parole for criminal mastermind "Doc" McCoy on the condition that he organises a bank robbery. The meticulously planned raid backfires, however, and McCoy and his wife are forced to race for freedom, chased by a group of gunmen and a sadistic killer.

REVIEW

In this gripping landmark thriller, ex-convict Steve McQueen and his wife Ali MacGraw head off to Mexico after a bank robbery backfires, pursued by crazed partner-in-crime Al Lettieri and the heavily armed henchmen of crime boss Ben Johnson. Directed by the master of screen violence, Sam Peckinpah, and scripted by Walter Hill from a novel by Jim Thompson, it's a modern western, a tough, disconcerting fable exploring the human soul, set in the barren landscapes of the Texan desert. The charismatic McQueen (who was only 50 when he died of a heart attack in 1980) has to face the unpalatable truth about how MacGraw secured his release from jail as their relationship – literally – comes under fire in a hail of bullets. In real life, the stars fell in love and subsequently married, but it wasn't to last.
ADRIAN TURNER

CAST

Steve McQueen *"Doc" McCoy* • Ali MacGraw *Carol McCoy* • Ben Johnson *Jack Benyon* • Sally Struthers *Fran Clinton* • Al Lettieri *Rudy Butler* • Slim Pickens *Cowboy* • Richard Bright *Thief* • Jack Dodson *Harold Clinton*

DIRECTOR

Sam Peckinpah

SCREENPLAY

Walter Hill, from the novel by Jim Thompson

DVD EXTRAS

Special Edition: commentary by DVD producer Nick Redman, authors Paul Seydor, Garner Simmons and David Weddle; "virtual" commentary with stills featuring Steve McQueen, Ali MacGraw and Sam Peckinpah; theatrical trailer. Also available on Blu-ray.

CONTENT ADVICE

Contains violence, swearing.

QUOTE UNQUOTE

Well, I just wouldn't worry about that, Doc, because I can always get you out. You know, I can screw every prison official in Texas if I have to! CAROL MCCOY

IF YOU ENJOYED THIS, WHY NOT TRY . . .
Bonnie and Clyde (1967)
Dollars (1971)

DID YOU KNOW?

Look out for the orange Volkswagen Beetle that Steve McQueen and Ali MacGraw speed past. It's being driven by actor James Garner, who happened to be visiting a buddy on the set and was offered a driving cameo by stuntman Carey Loftin.

Heat

CERTIFICATE: **15** | YEAR: **1995** | COUNTRY: **US** | **COLOUR** | RUNNING TIME: **163 MINUTES**

SYNOPSIS

Detective Vincent Hanna is closing in on notorious professional thief Neil McCauley and, after an armoured-car robbery goes spectacularly wrong, McCauley knows that the police are watching his every move. Even so, he decides to go ahead with one final heist before leaving the US for a new life.

REVIEW

Michael Mann's crime thriller about a cop (Al Pacino) and a robber (Robert De Niro) is epic in both scale and length, clocking in at just under three hours. Though punctuated by bursts of virtuoso action, including a running battle in downtown LA that ranks as one of the best action scenes ever filmed, it is the unusual emphasis on character that impresses most. De Niro is in fine form as the calm, methodical loner whose life is arranged so that he can abandon everything in 30 seconds when the heat is on, including his sidekick, Val Kilmer. Pacino, by contrast, is more of a cliché, angst-ridden and on his third marriage. Their scene together in the coffee shop makes us realise just how similar these two duellists are. It's only a pity that, after so much brilliance, Mann should succumb to a derivative ending – an airport chase, as per *Bullitt*, and a tidy if bloody resolution. **ADRIAN TURNER**

QUOTE UNQUOTE

I do what I do best, I take scores. You do what you do best, try to stop guys like me. **NEIL MCCAULEY**

IF YOU ENJOYED THIS, WHY NOT TRY ...

LA Takedown (1989)
Public Enemies (2009)

CAST

Al Pacino *Vincent Hanna* • Robert De Niro *Neil McCauley* • Val Kilmer *Chris Shiherlis* • Jon Voight *Nate* • Tom Sizemore *Michael Cheritto* • Diane Venora *Justine* • Amy Brenneman *Eady* • Ashley Judd *Charlene* • Mykelti Williamson *Drucker* • Wes Studi *Casals* • Natalie Portman *Lauren*

DIRECTOR

Michael Mann

SCREENPLAY

Michael Mann

DVD EXTRAS

Special Edition: commentary by Michael Mann; additional scenes; five origins and making-of documentaries; theatrical trailers.

DID YOU KNOW?

Al Pacino and Robert De Niro both starred in *The Godfather, Part II*, but never shared a scene until this film, which was promoted as their "showdown".

Hell Drivers

CERTIFICATE: **PG** | YEAR: **1957** | COUNTRY: **UK** | **BW** | RUNNING TIME: **103 MINUTES**

SYNOPSIS

Released from prison and seeking anonymity, Tom Yately takes a job with a firm of unscrupulous haulage contractors who stretch both drivers and regulations to the limit. Tom soon makes friends with the gregarious Gino and his sweetheart, Lucy, but finds himself at loggerheads with brutish foreman Red.

REVIEW

This gripping British thriller is given a cutting edge of social reality by blacklisted Hollywood director Cy Endfield. Stanley Baker stars as the ex-con driving lorries at perilous speeds to meet the deadlines of a haulage company, who uncovers a racket run by his unprincipled manager. There's a splendid performance from Patrick McGoohan as a lethal rival driver and a marvellous co-starring role for Herbert Lom (here, not playing the villain for a change). The supporting cast is also top class, a veritable Who's Who of British actors – Sid James, David McCallum, Gordon Jackson – who would go on to find fame on the big and the small screens, none more so than a young, pre-Bond Sean Connery. The truck sequences still have the power to thrill, and Endfield and his star Baker would go on to collaborate to even greater effect when they made *Zulu* together six years later. **TOM HUTCHINSON**

QUOTE UNQUOTE

If you think you're good enough to sit in my place, you have to prove it. **RED**

IF YOU ENJOYED THIS, WHY NOT TRY ...
Robbery (1967)
The Wages of Fear (1953)

CAST

Stanley Baker *Tom Yately* • Herbert Lom *Gino* • Peggy Cummins *Lucy* • Patrick McGoohan *Red* • William Hartnell *Cartley* • Wilfrid Lawson *Ed* • Sidney James *Dusty* • Jill Ireland *Jill* • Alfie Bass *Tinker* • Gordon Jackson *Scottie* • David McCallum *Jimmy Yately* • Sean Connery *Johnny*

DIRECTOR

C Raker Endfield [Cy Endfield]

SCREENPLAY

John Kruse, C Raker Endfield [Cy Endfield]

DVD EXTRAS

Special Edition: commentary by sound assistant Harry Fairbairn and journalist Andrew Robinson; theatrical trailer; commemorative booklet; original PR material; *Who Killed Lamb?* thriller starring Stanley Baker; news footage of Stanley Baker unveiling a plaque at his birthplace; two Stanley Baker interviews; *Return to the Rhondda* documentary featuring Stanley Baker from 1965; an episode of *Danger Man*; *The Stanley Baker Story*.

DID YOU KNOW?

Five of the cast went on to have iconic roles in the 1960s: Sean Connery in the Bond movies, Patrick McGoohan in *Danger Man* and *The Prisoner*, William Hartnell in *Doctor Who*, David McCallum in *The Man from UNCLE* and Sid James in the *Carry On* films.

A History of Violence

CERTIFICATE: **18** | YEAR: **2005** | COUNTRY: **US/GER** | **COLOUR** | RUNNING TIME: **91 MINUTES**

SYNOPSIS

Tom Stall has a quiet life running a diner in a small town. But his existence is thrown into chaos when he confronts two criminals who attack his customers. This act makes him a local hero, but it also sets in motion a chain of events that suggest Tom has a darker past than his neighbours realise.

REVIEW

Although he plays it surprisingly straight for once, director David Cronenberg nevertheless brings a dry wit and a satirical edge to this dark thriller. Life is sweet as apple pie for Tom Stall (Viggo Mortensen), his wife Edie (Maria Bello) and their regulation two kids. But when Tom becomes a media hero after preventing a hold-up, a disfigured thug (Ed Harris) surfaces with henchmen in tow. Insisting Tom is his old Mob buddy "Joey" from Philadelphia, he manages to cast doubt even in Edie's mind, creating a central "is-he-or-isn't-he" mystery that's deliciously teased out. Once that question is solved, the film sags slightly, but it perks up again in the final act thanks to a ripe comic turn from William Hurt. The violence comes in small but brutal bursts – the closest Cronenberg comes here to the horror that made his name in such films as *The Fly*. LESLIE FELPERIN

CAST

Viggo Mortensen *Tom Stall* • Maria Bello *Edie Stall* • William Hurt *Richie Cusack* • Ashton Holmes *Jack Stall* • Stephen McHattie *Leland Jones* • Peter MacNeill *Sheriff Sam Carney* • Ed Harris *Carl Fogarty* • Heidi Hayes *Sarah Stall* • Greg Bryk *William "Billy" Orser*

DIRECTOR

David Cronenberg

SCREENPLAY

Josh Olson, from the graphic novel by John Wagner, Vince Locke

DVD EXTRAS

Commentary by David Cronenberg; *Acts of Violence* making-of documentary; deleted scene with optional audio from Cronenberg; *The Unmaking of Scene* featurette; US version vs International version featurette; *Too Commercial for Cannes* featurette; original theatrical trailer. Also available on Blu-ray.

CONTENT ADVICE

Contains swearing, violence.

QUOTE UNQUOTE

You've got me mistaken for someone else. I'm not Joey Cusack! TOM STALL

IF YOU ENJOYED THIS, WHY NOT TRY . . .

Build My Gallows High (1947)
Eastern Promises (2007)

DID YOU KNOW?

The film is cited as being the last big Hollywood production to have received a proper release on VHS in the US.

The Hitcher

CERTIFICATE: **18** | YEAR: **1986** | COUNTRY: **US** | **COLOUR** | RUNNING TIME: **93 MINUTES**

SYNOPSIS

Young Jim Halsey is transporting a drive-away car from Chicago to San Diego, when he decides to give a lift to a hitch-hiker one rainy night. The soft-spoken stranger soon becomes violent, and though Jim manages to bundle the man out of the car, his trials and tribulations are only just beginning.

REVIEW

C Thomas Howell wishes he hadn't picked up seemingly harmless passenger Rutger Hauer in this feature debut from director Robert Harmon. That's because Hauer is a cold-blooded serial killer who quickly embroils Howell in a harrowing desert intrigue by framing him for his sick crimes. Chased by the police and shadowed by the enigmatic hitcher from hell, Howell's only support is a young waitress who believes his story. As played by Jennifer Jason Leigh, she adds some much-needed humanity along the way. Despite the film's huge lapses in logic and moments of wild self-parody, the plot twists generate considerable suspense and its surreal style has made it something of a cult classic. It was remade in 2007 with Sean Bean in the title role, but he found himself unable to top the inimitable Hauer. **ALAN JONES**

QUOTE UNQUOTE

I cut off his legs... and his arms... and his head. And I'm going to do the same to you. **JOHN RYDER**

IF YOU ENJOYED THIS, WHY NOT TRY ...

Detour (1945)
Dust Devil (1992)

CAST

Rutger Hauer *John Ryder* • C Thomas Howell *Jim Halsey* • Jennifer Jason Leigh *Nash* • Jeffrey DeMunn *Captain Esteridge*

DIRECTOR

Robert Harmon

SCREENPLAY

Eric Red

DVD EXTRAS

Special Edition: commentary by Eric Red, Robert Harmon; scene specific commentaries by C Thomas Howell, Edward S Feldman, Eric Red, Rutger Hauer, Mark Isham, John Seale, Robert Harmon; screenplay samples (including deleted scenes); *The Hitcher: How Do These Movies Get Made?* documentary; *China Lake* short movie with a written introduction from director Robert Harmon; *The Room* short movie with commentary by Rutger Hauer; filmographies; theatrical trailers.

CONTENT ADVICE

Contains violence, swearing.

DID YOU KNOW?

C Thomas Howell admitted that he was scared on and off the set by Rutger Hauer's intensity.

Insomnia

CERTIFICATE: **15** | YEAR: **2002** | COUNTRY: **US** | **COLOUR** | RUNNING TIME: **113 MINUTES**

SYNOPSIS

Troubled Los Angeles detective Will Dormer and his police partner Hap Eckhart fly to a remote Alaskan town to investigate the murder of a teenage girl. After accidentally killing Eckhart, Dormer is contacted by a man who admits to murdering the girl but wants a deal as he witnessed Eckhart's death.

REVIEW

Based on a 1997 Norwegian blockbuster of the same name, Christopher Nolan's masterfully directed psychodrama proves that hit European movies can be remade successfully. Alaska provides an arresting backdrop for this unhinged nightmare that sees hard-boiled LAPD detective Al Pacino (on dynamite form) sent to a small fishing town to help in a brutal homicide case. When he mistakenly kills his partner on a fudged stakeout and blames his quarry (Robin Williams) who saw what he did, the killer blackmails him into pinning both deaths on someone else. And so a cat-and-mouse game begins, with Pacino – terminally sleepless from the endless daylight – barely staying one-step ahead in the evidence-planting conspiracy. Dwelling on the far more compelling issues of ethical decay and moral breakdown than the whodunnit aspects, Nolan's inventive thriller is intensely gripping throughout. **ALAN JONES**

QUOTE UNQUOTE

It's all about small stuff. You know, small lies, small mistakes. People give themselves away, same in misdemeanours as they do on murder cases. It's just human nature. **WILL DORMER**

IF YOU ENJOYED THIS, WHY NOT TRY . . .

Insomnia (1997)

CAST

Al Pacino *Will Dormer* • Robin Williams *Walter Finch* • Hilary Swank *Ellie Burr* • Maura Tierney *Rachel Clement* • Martin Donovan *Hap Eckhart* • Nicky Katt *Fred Duggar* • Jonathan Jackson *Randy Stetz* • Paul Dooley *Chief Charles Nyback*

DIRECTOR

Christopher Nolan

SCREENPLAY

Hillary Seitz, from the 1997 film by Nikolaj Frobenius, Erik Skjoldbjaerg

DVD EXTRAS

Commentary by Christopher Nolan; commentary by Hilary Swank, Nathan Crowley, Dody Dorn, Wally Pfister, Hillary Seitz; conversation with Christopher Nolan, Al Pacino; making-of documentary; *In the Fog* with cinematographer Wally Pfister; *In the Fog* with production designer Nathan Crowley; *Eyes Wide Open* featurette on insomniacs; additional scene; stills gallery with music.

CONTENT ADVICE

Contains violence, swearing, nudity.

DID YOU KNOW?

Al Pacino is a longtime sufferer of chronic insomnia, so was the ideal choice to play a cop who is unable to sleep.

Internal Affairs

CERTIFICATE: **18** | YEAR: **1990** | COUNTRY: **US** | **COLOUR** | RUNNING TIME: **109 MINUTES**

SYNOPSIS

Los Angeles police officer Dennis Peck knows his way around the law. He can launder money, run a scam and even, for the right price, arrange a murder. But newly promoted internal affairs investigator Raymond Avilla isn't taken in by his dangerous charm, and time is beginning to run out for Peck.

REVIEW

In this gripping thriller from *Leaving Las Vegas* director Mike Figgis, Andy Garcia stars as an Internal Affairs investigator who's determined to prove that fellow Los Angeles police officer Richard Gere is corrupt with fingers in a lot of iffy pies. Gere – who had been on a run of critical and commercial flops in the late 1980s, despite the huge success of *An Officer and a Gentleman* in 1982 – is especially good as the dishonest and often violent policeman. Indeed, it's probably true to say that this is the movie that was responsible for reviving both his career and his leading man status. Gere's nastiness as the unscrupulous Peck is something of a revelation after years of pretty boy roles, and the vendetta that develops between him and the perpetually smouldering Garcia enthrals and repels in equal measure. **JOANNA BERRY**

CAST

Richard Gere *Dennis Peck* • Andy Garcia *Sergeant Raymond Avilla* • Nancy Travis *Kathleen Avilla* • Laurie Metcalf *Sergeant Amy Wallace* • Richard Bradford *Lieutenant Sergeant Grieb* • William Baldwin *Van Stretch*

DIRECTOR

Mike Figgis

SCREENPLAY

Henry Bean

CONTENT ADVICE

Contains violence, swearing, sex scenes.

QUOTE UNQUOTE

Go on, shoot her. She's a tramp. She's a big tramp. Your parents are dead, and you've got a tramp for a wife.
DENNIS PECK

IF YOU ENJOYED THIS, WHY NOT TRY . . .

Bad Lieutenant (1992)
Q & A (1990)

DID YOU KNOW?

Before becoming a film director, Mike Figgis played alongside a young Bryan Ferry in the rhythm and blues band Gas Board.

The Ipcress File

CERTIFICATE: **PG** | YEAR: **1965** | COUNTRY: **UK** | **COLOUR** | RUNNING TIME: **102 MINUTES**

SYNOPSIS

Intelligence agent Harry Palmer is plunged into the treacherous world of counter espionage as he investigates a bizarre "brain drain" among scientists after a boffin goes missing. Although there are leads to follow up, Palmer soon discovers that he can't trust anything – or anyone.

REVIEW

Len Deighton's first spy novel had everything except a name for its off-the-peg hero, so producer Harry Saltzman decided on Harry Palmer and cast the virtually unknown Michael Caine in this adaptation. Designed as a glamour-free counterpoint to the Bond movies (which Saltzman also co-produced), the story uncovers KGB operatives in the British Secret Service and allows our spy to talk Bermondsey, wear glasses and cook his own meals – things that Bond would never do. Instead of the *Orient Express*, it's the Central Line. But Saltzman was also cunning enough to engage Bond production design maestro Ken Adam, editor Peter Hunt and composer John Barry. There's some droll humour, energetic direction from Sidney J Furie (which sometimes shows us the world through Caine's own myopic eyes) and spot-on supporting performances by Guy Doleman and Nigel Green as bowler-hatted spooks.
ADRIAN TURNER

CAST
Michael Caine *Harry Palmer* • Nigel Green *Dalby* • Guy Doleman *Colonel Ross* • Sue Lloyd *Jean Courtney* • Gordon Jackson *Jock Carswell* • Aubrey Richards *Radcliffe* • Frank Gatliff *Bluejay/Grantby*

DIRECTOR
Sidney J Furie

SCREENPLAY
Bill Canaway, James Doran, from the novel by Len Deighton

AWARDS
Baftas (3): British Film, Cinematography (colour), Art Direction (colour)

DVD EXTRAS
Two-disc edition: commentary by Sidney Furie and editor Peter Hunt; *The Ipcress File: Michael Caine Goes Stella*; interview with production designer Ken Adam; *Candid Caine* TV documentary from 1969; theatrical trailer; stills gallery. Also available on Blu-ray.

CONTENT ADVICE
Contains swearing.

QUOTE UNQUOTE

You didn't come here to talk to me about button mushrooms and birds. **HARRY PALMER**

IF YOU ENJOYED THIS, WHY NOT TRY . . .
Funeral in Berlin (1966)
The Quiller Memorandum (1966)

DID YOU KNOW?
The acronym IPCRESS stands for "induction of psychoneuroses by conditioned reflex under stress".

JFK

CERTIFICATE: **15** | YEAR: **1991** | COUNTRY: **US** | **COLOUR AND BW** | RUNNING TIME: **188 MINUTES**

SYNOPSIS

On 22 November 1963, President Kennedy's death changes America for ever. Initially, a saddened nation is satisfied with the guilt of Lee Harvey Oswald. But, as the years pass, unease and cynicism set in. New Orleans prosecutor Jim Garrison is convinced of a conspiracy, and sets out to prove it.

REVIEW

It's pretty clear that, with the assassination of John F Kennedy, director Oliver Stone takes his self-appointed position as the chronicler of recent US history far too seriously to be objective. Yet, before you dismiss this review as just another tirade against Stone and star Kevin Costner, let's remember that the cover-up theory has lost none of its fascination more than 40 years after the event. Whether you believe Lee Harvey Oswald acted alone or whether you adhere to another theory, this is a persuasively staged conspiracy thriller. What's so remarkable is how deftly Stone conveys such a wealth of information and how he manages to ensure that every character makes an impact, no matter how short their screen time. The Oscar-winning photography and editing are superb, and the ensemble is a triumph of casting. **DAVID PARKINSON**

QUOTE UNQUOTE

Who killed Kennedy! It's a mystery! It's a mystery wrapped in a riddle inside an enigma! The f***in' shooters don't even know! Don't you get it? **DAVID FERRIE**

IF YOU ENJOYED THIS, WHY NOT TRY . . .

The Manchurian Candidate (1962)
Winter Kills (1979)

CAST

Kevin Costner *Jim Garrison* • Sissy Spacek *Liz Garrison* • Joe Pesci *David Ferrie* • Tommy Lee Jones *Clay Shaw* • Gary Oldman *Lee Harvey Oswald* • Jay O Sanders *Lou Ivon* • Michael Rooker *Bill Broussard* • Laurie Metcalf *Susie Cox* • Gary Grubbs *Al Oser* • John Candy *Dean Andrews* • Jack Lemmon *Jack Martin* • Walter Matthau *Senator Russell Long* • Ed Asner [Edward Asner] *Guy Bannister* • Donald Sutherland *Colonel X* • Kevin Bacon *Willie O'Keefe* • Brian Doyle-Murray *Jack Ruby*

DIRECTOR

Oliver Stone

SCREENPLAY

Oliver Stone, Zachary Sklar, from the non-fiction book *On the Trail of the Assassins* by Jim Garrison, from the non-fiction book *Crossfire: the Plot That Killed Kennedy* by Jim Marrs

AWARDS

Academy Awards (2): Cinematography, Editing
Baftas (2): Editing, Sound

DVD EXTRAS

Two versions available on DVD: the theatrical release and a two-disc director's cut. Neither has any extras.

CONTENT ADVICE

Contains drug abuse, swearing, violence.

DID YOU KNOW?

Director Oliver Stone has a cameo role as the Secret Service agent who runs to the back of the limousine following the assassination.

When a murder case
is this shocking, which do you trust?

Your emotions or your evidence?

JAGGED EDGE

COLUMBIA PICTURES PRESENTS

A MARTIN RANSOHOFF PRODUCTION

A RICHARD MARQUAND FILM GLENN CLOSE

JEFF BRIDGES "JAGGED EDGE" PETER COYOTE ROBERT LOGGIA MUSIC BY JOHN BARRY

WRITTEN BY JOE ESZTERHAS PRODUCED BY MARTIN RANSOHOFF DIRECTED BY RICHARD MARQUAND

Jagged Edge

CERTIFICATE: **18** | YEAR: **1985** | COUNTRY: **US** | **COLOUR** | RUNNING TIME: **104 MINUTES**

SYNOPSIS

A beautiful, wealthy heiress has been found brutally stabbed to death, the murder weapon a serrated hunting knife; her husband, Jack Forrester, is accused of the killing. Defence lawyer Teddy Barnes is hired to represent him at a harrowing public trial, and begins to fall for her charming client.

REVIEW

Because writer Joe Eszterhas has continually reworked the same basic formula (hero/heroine falls for murder suspect), it's easy to forget how startling the scenario was when it was first employed in this compelling thriller. Glenn Close plays the defence attorney haunted by a case from her past when the wrong man went to jail, who falls in love with her latest client (Jeff Bridges), a charming publisher accused of brutally murdering his wealthy wife using a large hunting knife with a serrated blade. Director Richard Marquand never misses a beat, gleefully tossing in red herrings and keeping us guessing until the end. There are expert support turns from Peter Coyote as the assistant DA and a foul-mouthed Robert Loggia as the defence team's investigator, and it remains an enthralling, if a tad incredible, ride. **JOHN FERGUSON**

QUOTE UNQUOTE

He picked that woman very carefully. He knew she played tennis with Slade. He planned this for eighteen months. He is not a psychopath. He's an iceman... he's a monster!
THOMAS KRASNY

IF YOU ENJOYED THIS, WHY NOT TRY . . .

Primal Fear (1996)
Suspect (1987)

CAST

Jeff Bridges *Jack Forrester* • Glenn Close *Teddy Barnes* • Peter Coyote *Thomas Krasny* • Robert Loggia *Sam Ransom* • John Dehner *Judge Carrigan* • Lance Henriksen *Frank Martin* • Leigh Taylor-Young *Virginia Howell* • Marshall Colt *Bobby Slade*

DIRECTOR

Richard Marquand

SCREENPLAY

Joe Eszterhas

DVD EXTRAS

Theatrical trailer; filmographies.

CONTENT ADVICE

Contains violence, swearing, brief nudity.

DID YOU KNOW?

Kevin Costner is thought to have refused the role of Jack Forrester.

Jaws

CERTIFICATE: **PG** | YEAR: **1975** | COUNTRY: **US** | **COLOUR** | RUNNING TIME: **118 MINUTES**

SYNOPSIS

The Atlantic resort of Amity Island is preparing for its lucrative summer season when death strikes in the form of a great white shark attack. With his community facing financial disaster if the tourist hordes are scared away, Mayor Vaughn orders police chief Brody to keep the beaches open.

REVIEW

This tale of a great white shark terrorising a New England resort community and the modern-day Captain Ahab (Robert Shaw) employed to kill it is a classic of the suspense thriller genre. It's also credited with creating the summer blockbuster craze that Hollywood pins its financial hopes on every year. Director Steven Spielberg creates maximum suspense in the first dark moments and then maintains the momentum with brilliant sleight-of-hand direction, turning Peter Benchley's pulp novel into the scariest sea saga ever filmed. John Williams's oh-so-simple Oscar-winning music was laughed out of the room when first demonstrated to Spielberg, yet it dominates the movie. And the excellent performances of Roy Scheider as the police chief who's afraid of the water and Richard Dreyfuss as the shark expert add to the ingeniously mounted tension that cleverly plays on all our deepest primeval fears. **ALAN JONES**

QUOTE UNQUOTE

You're gonna need a bigger boat. **BRODY**

IF YOU ENJOYED THIS, WHY NOT TRY . . .

Deep Blue Sea (1999)
Lake Placid (1999)
Mission of the Shark (1991)

CAST

Roy Scheider *Brody* • Robert Shaw *Quint* • Richard Dreyfuss *Hooper* • Lorraine Gary *Ellen Brody* • Murray Hamilton *Vaughn* • Carl Gottlieb *Meadows* • Jeffrey C Kramer [Jeffrey Kramer] *Hendricks* • Susan Backlinie *Chrissie* • Jonathan Filley *Cassidy*

DIRECTOR

Steven Spielberg

SCREENPLAY

Peter Benchley, Carl Gottlieb, Howard Sackler, from the novel by Peter Benchley

AWARDS

Academy Awards (3): Editing, Original Score, Sound
Baftas (1): Score

DVD EXTRAS

30th Anniversary Special Edition: deleted scenes; outtakes; *A Look inside Jaws* behind-the-scenes documentary; an on-set interview with Steven Spielberg from 1974; interactive 3D great white shark and facts about the ocean-dweller; stills gallery; storyboard to finished film comparison.

CONTENT ADVICE

Contains violence, swearing, nudity.

DID YOU KNOW?

The animatronic shark became so troublesome that Steven Spielberg dubbed it the "great white turd".

The Killers

CERTIFICATE: **PG** | YEAR: **1946** | COUNTRY: **US** | **BW** | RUNNING TIME: **98 MINUTES**

SYNOPSIS

Ole "Swede" Anderson waits in a boarding-house room for his inevitable death at the hands of two hitmen. It's left to insurance investigator Jim Reardon to uncover the dead man's story – a bitter tale of his downward spiral into crime and betrayal at the hands of a beautiful woman.

REVIEW

This is one of the most powerful and influential thrillers ever made, with director Robert Siodmak's lovingly bleak and pessimistic tone virtually defining the term *film noir*. Based on a short story of remarkable power by Ernest Hemingway, the movie opens with a murder and then seeks, through intricate flashbacks, to explain why the victim was so accepting – welcoming, even – of his fate. Burt Lancaster, all coiled anger as the fall guy, makes a stunning film debut and there's a career-defining role for Ava Gardner as the *femme fatale*. In fact, there's class all round: the Edward Hopper-influenced design is brilliantly atmospheric, Miklos Rozsa's superb score was so effective it was re-used for TV's *Dragnet* and John Huston had a hand in the taut screenplay. The Don Siegel remake in 1964 isn't a patch on this marvellous original. TONY SLOMAN

CAST

Burt Lancaster *Ole "Swede" Anderson/ Pete Lunn* • Ava Gardner *Kitty Collins* • Edmond O'Brien *Jim Reardon* • Albert Dekker *Big Jim Colfax* • Sam Levene *Lieutenant Sam Lubinsky* • Charles D Brown *Packy Robinson* • Donald MacBride *Kenyon* • Phil Brown *Nick Adams* • Charles McGraw *Al* • William Conrad *Max* • Vince Barnett *Charleston*

DIRECTOR

Robert Siodmak

SCREENPLAY

Anthony Veiller, John Huston, from a short story by Ernest Hemingway

QUOTE UNQUOTE

I'm poison, Swede, to myself and everybody around me.
KITTY COLLINS

IF YOU ENJOYED THIS, WHY NOT TRY . . .

The Killers (1964)

DID YOU KNOW?

When producer Mark Hellinger saw the rushes featuring the film debut of former circus performer Burt Lancaster as the Swede, he was so happy he shouted "so help me, may all my actors be acrobats."

Kiss Me Deadly

CERTIFICATE: **12** | YEAR: **1955** | COUNTRY: **US** | **BW** | RUNNING TIME: **103 MINUTES**

SYNOPSIS

Private eye Mike Hammer picks up a terrified hitch-hiker who says she has escaped from a Los Angeles asylum. They are then run off the road by a mysterious car and the girl is tortured and killed. But Hammer survives to follow a trail of extortion and violence that leads to an explosive secret.

REVIEW

This early feature by *Dirty Dozen* director Robert Aldrich made him both a name in arty circles (the critics of *Cahiers du Cinéma* loved him and the film) and a formidable presence in cinema. He took a piece of Mickey Spillane "pulp" fiction and turned it into an astonishing fable, with Pandora's Box transformed into a nuclear furnace. The look is off-the-wall stylish and the tension builds to a climax that is near-apocalyptic. Everything is on the side of the unexpected from the opening credits to the fact that Spillane's detective Mike Hammer (Ralph Meeker) is a flawed (and brutal) antihero who finds himself in over his head after picking up a girl on the run. Albert Dekker is a classily obnoxious villain, but it's the women you have to watch. As the title suggests, their embrace is deadly.

TOM HUTCHINSON

CAST

Ralph Meeker *Mike Hammer* • Albert Dekker *Dr Soberin* • Paul Stewart *Carl Evello* • Maxine Cooper *Velda* • Gaby Rodgers *Gabrielle/Lily Carver* • Wesley Addy *Pat Chambers* • Juano Hernandez *Eddie Yeager* • Nick Dennis *Nick* • Cloris Leachman *Christina Bailey/Berga Torn*

DIRECTOR

Robert Aldrich

SCREENPLAY

Al Bezzerides, from the novel by Mickey Spillane

DVD EXTRAS

Theatrical trailer.

QUOTE UNQUOTE

If we don't make that bus stop... If we don't... remember me. **CHRISTINA**

IF YOU ENJOYED THIS, WHY NOT TRY . . .
Farewell, My Lovely (1975)

DID YOU KNOW?

If you want to know where Quentin Tarantino got the "What's in the suitcase?" idea for *Pulp Fiction*, look no further than this classic *film noir*.

jane fonda · donald sutherland

Lots
of guys
swing with
a call girl
like Bree.

One guy just
wants to
kill her.

an alan j. pakula production

'klute'

Klute

CERTIFICATE: **18** | YEAR: **1971** | COUNTRY: **US** | **COLOUR** | RUNNING TIME: **107 MINUTES**

SYNOPSIS

Small-town private eye John Klute is hired to investigate the disappearance of a scientist who's been missing from his Pennsylvania home town for six months. In New York, he becomes involved with call-girl Bree Daniels, who has links to the missing man and is being stalked by an unhinged former client.

REVIEW

Jane Fonda deservedly won the best actress Oscar for her performance in this exceptional film from director Alan J Pakula, taking a remarkable walk on the wild side as troubled call girl Bree Daniels, who's being stalked by a homicidal maniac. Donald Sutherland is on top form, too, playing gentle small-town private eye John Klute, who teaches Bree the difference between love and sex as he closes in on the killer. Fonda and Sutherland interact beautifully, but nothing can match the superb improvised scenes between Fonda's character and her psychiatrist in which she explores her attraction to prostitution. Genuine nail-biting suspense is generated thanks to a spine-tingling score by Michael Small and the atmospheric cinematography of *Godfather* cameraman Gordon Willis, who makes wonderful use of claustrophobic, shadowy interiors as Klute lays his trap for the killer. **ALAN JONES**

CAST

Jane Fonda *Bree Daniels* • Donald Sutherland *John Klute* • Charles Cioffi *Peter Cable* • Nathan George *Lieutenant Trask* • Roy R Scheider [Roy Scheider] *Frank Ligourin* • Dorothy Tristan *Arlyn Page* • Rita Gam *Trina* • Vivian Nathan *Psychiatrist*

DIRECTOR

Alan J Pakula

SCREENPLAY

Andy Lewis, Dave Lewis

AWARDS

Academy Awards (1): Actress (Jane Fonda)

CONTENT ADVICE

Contains swearing, nudity.

QUOTE UNQUOTE

Men would pay $200 for me, and here you are turning down a freebie. **BREE DANIELS**

IF YOU ENJOYED THIS, WHY NOT TRY ...

Sea of Love (1989)

DID YOU KNOW?

The apartment occupied by Jane Fonda in the movie was constructed with a real toilet so that Fonda could spend as much time as possible on set to replicate call-girl Bree's sense of detachment from New York City life.

The Lady Vanishes

CERTIFICATE: **U** | YEAR: **1938** | COUNTRY: **UK** | **BW** | RUNNING TIME: **92 MINUTES**

SYNOPSIS

Iris Henderson's Tyrolean holiday is over and she is going home to be married. On the London-bound train she is befriended by the kindly Miss Froy, but when Iris awakes after a nap, the lady has vanished – her fellow passengers claim she never existed. Who can Iris trust, and who has Miss Froy?

REVIEW

Considered by most critics to be a close second behind *The 39 Steps* as the best film of Alfred Hitchcock's British period, this sublime comedy thriller was apparently acclaimed French director François Truffaut's favourite of Hitch's films. It's also said that Orson Welles watched it no less than eight times. Co-scripted by Alma Reville (Mrs Hitchcock) and the dynamic duo of Frank Launder and Sidney Gilliat, the film doesn't have a single wasted frame, as Michael Redgrave and Margaret Lockwood search a Balkan express train for dotty Dame May Whitty as it steams towards London. Basil Radford and Naunton Wayne drew all the plaudits as the cricket-mad Charters and Caldicott, but the support playing of Paul Lukas, Mary Clare and Cecil Parker is also first class. Hitchcock cameo fans should keep their eyes peeled during the London station scene. **DAVID PARKINSON**

CAST

Margaret Lockwood *Iris Henderson* • Michael Redgrave *Gilbert* • Paul Lukas *Dr Hartz* • Dame May Whitty *Miss Froy* • Cecil Parker *Eric Todhunter* • Linden Travers *"Mrs" Todhunter* • Naunton Wayne *Caldicott* • Basil Radford *Charters* • Mary Clare *Baroness* • Googie Withers *Blanche*

DIRECTOR

Alfred Hitchcock

SCREENPLAY

Sidney Gilliat, Frank Launder, Alma Reville, from the novel *The Wheel Spins* by Ethel Lina White

DVD EXTRAS

Special Edition: introduction by writer and film historian Charles Barr; image gallery; original theatrical trailer; facsimile of script.

QUOTE UNQUOTE

Well, I don't see how a thing like cricket can make you forget seeing people. **IRIS HENDERSON**

IF YOU ENJOYED THIS, WHY NOT TRY . . .
Flightplan (2005)
Night Train to Munich (1940)

DID YOU KNOW?

The claustrophobic atmosphere of the train carriage was all too real for the actors, as the set it was filmed on was just 90ft in length.

The Last Seduction

CERTIFICATE: **18** | YEAR: **1993** | COUNTRY: **US** | **COLOUR** | RUNNING TIME: **105 MINUTES**

SYNOPSIS

Clay Gregory pulls off a drugs deal, then returns to his beautiful, ruthless wife Bridget with the proceeds. He takes a shower, she takes the money and the chase is on. Bridget hides out in a small town where the hapless Mike falls for her cool lies, unaware he's just part of an elaborate plan.

REVIEW

John Dahl secured his reputation as one of the hottest directors of the 1990s with this cool-as-ice, wantonly playful, bitter-and-twisted excursion into neon-shaded contemporary *film noir*. At its commanding centre is sizzling and smouldering Linda Fiorentino in a star-making role as the man-eating *femme fatale* from hell. As gorgeous go-getter Bridget Gregory, she swaps dirty talk for dirty deeds when she cons husband Bill Pullman into doing a big drugs deal, only to run off with the money. Hiding out in a small town, the manipulative mantrap changes identity, gets a new job and seduces besotted insurance agent Peter Berg into carrying out her every whim. Then she sets him up as the pawn in a daring game of double-cross. This sassy and superior suspense thriller is a must-see – pulp fiction rarely comes as well-appointed or as absorbingly clever. **ALAN JONES**

CAST

Linda Fiorentino *Bridget Gregory* • Peter Berg *Mike Swale* • Bill Pullman *Clay Gregory* • JT Walsh *Frank Griffith* • Bill Nunn *Harlan* • Herb Mitchell *Bob Trotter* • Brien Varady *Chris* • Dean Norris *Shep* • Donna Wilson *Stacy*

DIRECTOR

John Dahl

SCREENPLAY

Steve Barancik

DVD EXTRAS

Two-disc Special Edition: theatrical version of the film, plus an extended director's cut with deleted scene insertions; commentary by John Dahl; *The Art of Seduction* documentary about the making of the film; booklet written by Dr Linda Ruth Williams, author of *The Erotic Thriller in Contemporary Society*; an episode from TV series *Fallen Angels* entitled *Tomorrow I Die*, starring Kim Coates, Heather Graham, Bill Pullman; stills gallery; theatrical trailer.

CONTENT ADVICE

Contains violence, swearing, sex scenes, nudity.

QUOTE UNQUOTE

Anyone check you for a heartbeat recently? **FRANK GRIFFITH**

IF YOU ENJOYED THIS, WHY NOT TRY...

Bound (1996)
Ossessione (1942)

DID YOU KNOW?

When Bill Pullman taught theatre at Montana State University, *The Last Seduction* director John Dahl was one of his students.

Laura

CERTIFICATE: **PG** | YEAR: **1944** | COUNTRY: **US** | **BW** | RUNNING TIME: **83 MINUTES**

SYNOPSIS

Detective Mark McPherson is investigating the brutal murder of a beautiful young woman, and interviewing suspects that include a sardonic newspaper columnist and a debonair playboy. As he searches for the killer, he learns more about the victim, Laura, and finds himself strangely attracted to her.

REVIEW

"I shall never forget the night Laura died... " begins the narrator, and neither will you. This taut romantic mystery, in which New York detective Dana Andrews falls in love with an image, encapsulates what *film noir* is all about. Otto Preminger's moody, stark direction is greatly helped by the casting of beautiful Gene Tierney in the title role (after Jennifer Jones turned it down), a southern-accented Vincent Price as a smarmy gigolo and the incomparable Clifton Webb as columnist Waldo Lydecker. The David Raksin score with its haunting "Laura Theme" is, quite simply, matchless (and was apparently inspired by a letter the composer received from his wife). If you've never seen it, don't miss, and don't be put off by the film's now classic status – it's a rattling good thriller and bears watching time and time again. **TONY SLOMAN**

QUOTE UNQUOTE

In my case, self-absorption is completely justified. I have never discovered any other subject quite so worthy of my attention. **WALDO LYDECKER**

IF YOU ENJOYED THIS, WHY NOT TRY . . .

Gilda (1946)
Rebecca (1940)

CAST

Gene Tierney *Laura Hunt* • Dana Andrews *Det Mark McPherson* • Clifton Webb *Waldo Lydecker* • Vincent Price *Shelby Carpenter* • Judith Anderson *Ann Treadwell* • Dorothy Adams *Bessie Clary* • James Flavin *McAvity* • Clyde Fillmore *Bullitt* • Ralph Dunn *Fred Callahan* • Grant Mitchell *Corey* • Kathleen Howard *Louise* • Lee Tung Foo *Servant* • Cy Kendall *Inspector*

DIRECTOR

Otto Preminger

SCREENPLAY

Jay Dratler, Samuel Hoffenstein, Betty Reinhardt, Jerome Cady, from the novel by Vera Caspary

AWARDS

Academy Awards (1): Cinematography (black and white)

DVD EXTRAS

Two-disc *Cinema Reserve* edition: commentary by composer David Raksin and film historian Jeanine Basinger; commentary by film historian Rudy Behlmer; extended scene; *The Obsession* documentary; *Gene Tierney: a Shattered Portrait* documentary; *Vincent Price: the Versatile Villain* documentary; trailer.

DID YOU KNOW?

The famous portrait of Laura seen throughout the film is actually an enlarged photograph overlaid with oil paint.

Leon

CERTIFICATE: **18** | YEAR: **1994** | COUNTRY: **FR** | **COLOUR** | RUNNING TIME: **110 MINUTES**

SYNOPSIS

In Little Italy, New York, 12-year-old Mathilda witnesses the murder of her family by a corrupt DEA agent. Escaping the carnage, she seeks refuge in the apartment of a neighbour, Leon, an illiterate hitman. In the coming weeks, they forge a powerful relationship as Mathilda plans her revenge.

REVIEW

Funny, tragic and brilliant, French director Luc Besson's first American-set movie is a haunting thriller that explores the relationship between the emotionally stunted hitman of the title and his 12-year-old neighbour, Mathilda. The illiterate Sicilian loner (played by Jean Reno) is reluctantly forced to befriend and protect the girl (Natalie Portman in her breakthrough role) after her family is wiped out by a corrupt cop (Gary Oldman). Leon ends up teaching Mathilda the tricks of his trade so she can take revenge. Reno and Portman intelligently convey how Leon's carefully constructed, reclusive existence falls apart as he lets feelings enter his life for the first time. But it's Besson's visual flair that sets the film apart. Ultra-stylish action scenes and breathtaking set pieces are interspersed with provocative dark humour to propel *Leon* into the suspense stratosphere. **ALAN JONES**

QUOTE UNQUOTE

Bonnie and Clyde didn't work alone. Thelma and Louise didn't work alone. And they were the best. **MATHILDA**

IF YOU ENJOYED THIS, WHY NOT TRY ...

Gloria (1980)
Road to Perdition (2002)

CAST

Jean Reno *Leon* • Gary Oldman *Stansfield* • Natalie Portman *Mathilda* • Danny Aiello *Tony* • Michael Badalucco *Mathilda's father* • Peter Appel *Malky* • Ellen Greene *Mathilda's mother*

DIRECTOR

Luc Besson

SCREENPLAY

Luc Besson

DVD EXTRAS

Director's Cut: documentary *The Road to Leon*; 10-year making-of retrospective; *Natalie Portman: Staying Young*; theatrical trailer. Also available on Blu-ray.

CONTENT ADVICE

Contains violence, swearing.

DID YOU KNOW?

The interior footage of Leon's apartment was shot in Paris; the corridor sequences were completed a month earlier in New York.

Lost Highway

CERTIFICATE: **18** | YEAR: **1996** | COUNTRY: **US** | **COLOUR** | RUNNING TIME: **128 MINUTES**

SYNOPSIS

Jazz saxophonist Fred Madison receives a series of videotapes showing the interior of the house he shares with his wife Renee. As the tapes become increasingly menacing and filled with violence, Fred is plagued by nightmarish visions of a mystery man and, finally, accused of his wife's murder.

REVIEW

Four years after the *Twin Peaks* phenomenon, David Lynch came up with this narrative-defying psychological thriller about a jazz saxophonist (an exemplary Bill Pullman) in a disturbed domestic limbo, who suddenly and inexplicably transforms into a younger man (Balthazar Getty). Though never together in a scene, the men share what appears to be the same elusive, deceptive woman (Patricia Arquette in contrasting wigs). It's not the most accessible scenario, but the delivery is hypnotising. And, while other modern films about bad people, paranoia and deceptive women get labelled *film noir*, Lynch reinvents the form rather than just relying on its storyline formula. Painterly, impenetrable and creepy, but never consciously hip, this is a painful, nightmarish vision of suffering and yearning that echoes Hitchcock's *Vertigo*. **DAVID OPPEDISANO**

CAST

Bill Pullman *Fred Madison* • Patricia Arquette *Renee Madison/Alice Wakefield* • Balthazar Getty *Pete Dayton* • Robert Blake *Mystery man* • Natasha Gregson Wagner *Sheila* • Robert Loggia *Mr Eddy/Dick Laurent* • Gary Busey *Bill Dayton* • Richard Pryor *Arnie* • Michael Massee *Andy* • Henry Rollins *Guard Henry* • Jack Nance *Phil* • Mink Stole *Forewoman* • Giovanni Ribisi *Steve "V"*

DIRECTOR

David Lynch

SCREENPLAY

David Lynch, Barry Gifford

DVD EXTRAS

Two-disc Special Edition: Interviews with David Lynch, Bill Pullman, Robert Loggia, Patricia Arquette; making-of featurette; trailers.

CONTENT ADVICE

Contains violence, swearing, sex scenes, nudity.

QUOTE UNQUOTE

I like to remember things my own way... How I remember them. Not necessarily the way they happened. **FRED MADISON**

IF YOU ENJOYED THIS, WHY NOT TRY ...

Hidden (2005)
Vanishing Point (1971)

DID YOU KNOW?

David Lynch says the subconscious inspiration behind the film was the OJ Simpson trial.

The Maltese Falcon

CERTIFICATE: **PG** | YEAR: **1941** | COUNTRY: **US** | **BW** | RUNNING TIME: **96 MINUTES**

SYNOPSIS

Hired by the mysterious, alluring and plainly deceitful Brigid O'Shaughnessy, laconic San Francisco private eye Sam Spade finds himself entangled in a murderous conspiracy that centres on a nefarious bunch of characters who will stop at nothing to get their hands on a priceless black statuette.

REVIEW

This third version of Dashiell Hammett's hard-boiled crime drama is superb cinematic entertainment. It created a brand-new movie icon in Humphrey Bogart's cynical private eye, Sam Spade, bringing him richly deserved stardom after years of toil in supporting parts. It was also the beginning of a beautiful friendship between Bogie and John Huston, who was then a screenwriter making his feature debut as director, and whose tart screenplay retains most of the sharp dialogue and sleazy amorality of Hammett's original. The supporting cast couldn't be bettered – stage actor Sydney Greenstreet made his screen debut as Gutman; Peter Lorre is the whiny, effeminate Joel Cairo; Mary Astor is cast against type as *femme fatale* supreme Brigid O'Shaughnessy. Watch, too, for Huston's father Walter as a ship's officer, and admire the pace and panache generated by the Warner Bros production team. **TONY SLOMAN**

QUOTE UNQUOTE

If you kill me, how are you gonna get the bird? **SAM SPADE**

IF YOU ENJOYED THIS, WHY NOT TRY . . .

The Asphalt Jungle (1950)
Hammett (1982)

■

CAST

Humphrey Bogart *Samuel Spade* • Mary Astor *Brigid O'Shaughnessy/Miss Wonderly* • Gladys George *Iva Archer* • Peter Lorre *Joel Cairo* • Barton MacLane *Lt of Detectives Dundy* • Lee Patrick *Effie Perine* • Sydney Greenstreet *Kasper Gutman* • Ward Bond *Det Tom Polhaus* • Jerome Cowan *Miles Archer* • Elisha Cook Jr *Wilmer Cook*

DIRECTOR

John Huston

SCREENPLAY

John Huston, from the novel by Dashiell Hammett

DVD EXTRAS

Two-disc Special Edition: commentary by Bogart biographer Eric Lax; Oscar-nominated short *The Gay Parisian*; classic cartoon *Hiawatha's Rabbit Hunt*; *The Maltese Falcon: One Magnificent Bird* documentary; blooper reel; trailers.

DID YOU KNOW?

Gutman and Wilmer's nicknames, "Fat Man" and "Little Boy", were used for the bombs dropped on Nagasaki and Hiroshima four years later.

The Manchurian Candidate

CERTIFICATE: **15** | YEAR: **1962** | COUNTRY: **US** | **BW** | RUNNING TIME: **130 MINUTES**

SYNOPSIS

Sergeant Raymond Shaw returns from the Korean War a hero, but his fellow soldiers' memories of his bravery seem vague. When the commander of his platoon, Bennett Marco, begins to suffer from inexplicable nightmares, he begins his own investigation into exactly what happened during the conflict.

REVIEW

Laurence Harvey is brilliantly cast and wonderfully creepy as the war hero brainwashed by Korean communists in this fearfully prophetic thriller. Frank Sinatra plays Harvey's former comrade who tries to establish the truth, and Angela Lansbury is Harvey's utterly terrifying mother (she was only three years older than him in real life). Co-written by George Axelrod and director John Frankenheimer from Richard Condon's novel and photographed in crisp black and white, this blackly comic and suspenseful film ranks with Stanley Kubrick's *Dr Strangelove* as one of the toughest and most original movies of the 1960s. It also puts a whole new spin on the innocent pastime of solitaire. Following President Kennedy's assassination in 1963, Sinatra had the film withdrawn from distribution for many years. It was remade in 2004, starring Denzel Washington and Meryl Streep. **ADRIAN TURNER**

CAST

Frank Sinatra *Bennett Marco* • Laurence Harvey *Raymond Shaw* • Janet Leigh *Rosie* • Angela Lansbury *Raymond's mother* • Henry Silva *Chunjim* • James Gregory *Senator John Iselin* • Leslie Parrish *Jocie Jordon* • John McGiver *Senator Thomas Jordon*

DIRECTOR

John Frankenheimer

SCREENPLAY

George Axelrod, John Frankenheimer, from the novel by Richard Condon

DVD EXTRAS

Commentary by John Frankenheimer; interview with Frank Sinatra, George Axelrod, John Frankenheimer; trivia, production notes; theatrical trailer.

QUOTE UNQUOTE

It's a terrible thing to hate your mother, but I didn't always hate her. When I was a child, I only kind of disliked her. **RAYMOND SHAW**

IF YOU ENJOYED THIS, WHY NOT TRY . . .

The Manchurian Candidate (2004)
Telefon (1977)

■

DID YOU KNOW?

The presidential assassination plot was causing United Artists unease until – as a favor to Frank Sinatra – soon-to-be-assassinated President John F Kennedy called to OK the production.

Manhunter

CERTIFICATE: **18** | YEAR: **1986** | COUNTRY: **US** | **COLOUR** | RUNNING TIME: **114 MINUTES**

SYNOPSIS

Ex-FBI investigator Will Graham is called in to solve a series of brutal murders by a killer dubbed the "Tooth Fairy". To help him in his search, Graham calls on the imprisoned Dr Hannibal Lecktor, a brilliant psychotherapist with a talent for manipulation and a taste for human flesh.

REVIEW

Whether or not, as some critics contend, this is a better movie than the multi-Oscar-winning *The Silence of the Lambs* (the second and more celebrated film adaptation of novelist Thomas Harris's source material), it is undoubtedly a gripping psycho-chiller in its own right. *CSI's* William Petersen plays the lonely, sleep-deprived former FBI whizz, hauled from retirement to help hunt down a sophisticated serial murderer called Francis Dollarhyde, nicknamed the "Tooth Fairy". Strong performances, especially from Brian Cox as manipulative cannibal Hannibal Lecktor and the imposing Tom Noonan as Dollarhyde, combine with clever plot details (Dollarhyde's strangely moving relationship with Joan Allen's blind woman is particularly memorable) and top-notch direction by Michael Mann to produce an atmospheric and arresting thriller. **PETER FREEDMAN**

QUOTE UNQUOTE

Have you ever seen blood in the moonlight, Will? It appears quite black. **DR HANNIBAL LECKTOR**

IF YOU ENJOYED THIS, WHY NOT TRY . . .

Red Dragon (2002)
Zodiac (2007)

CAST

William Petersen [William L Petersen] *Will Graham* • Brian Cox *Dr Hannibal Lecktor* • Dennis Farina *Jack Crawford* • Kim Greist *Molly Graham* • Stephen Lang *Freddie Lounds* • Tom Noonan *Francis Dollarhyde* • Joan Allen *Reba* • Benjamin Hendrickson *Dr Chilton*

DIRECTOR

Michael Mann

SCREENPLAY

Michael Mann, from the novel *Red Dragon* by Thomas Harris

DVD EXTRAS

Two-disc Special Edition: *The Manhunter Look* documentary; *Inside Manhunter* documentary; photo gallery; trailers; an additional remastered director's cut of the film with two minutes of restored footage and a commentary by Michael Mann.

CONTENT ADVICE

Contains violence, swearing.

DID YOU KNOW?

The "prison" where Hannibal Lecktor is being held is in fact the High Museum of Art in Atlanta, Georgia.

Marathon Man

CERTIFICATE: **18** | YEAR: **1976** | COUNTRY: **US** | **COLOUR** | RUNNING TIME: **119 MINUTES**

SYNOPSIS

Following the murder of his government agent brother, New York college student and would-be marathon runner Babe Levy becomes caught up in a deadly plot involving a cache of priceless gems and the sinister Dr Szell, an infamous Nazi known as the "White Angel of Auschwitz".

REVIEW

Dustin Hoffman stars as the bewildered New York student training to run a marathon who inadvertently becomes mixed up in a hunt for a hoard of Nazi diamonds in this gripping thriller from director John Schlesinger, adapted by William Goldman from his own novel. Laurence Olivier is the essence of evil as the former concentration camp sadist who leaves his hiding place in South America to claim his legacy – the priceless gems taken from Jewish victims during the war. Also making an impact is Roy Scheider as Hoffman's secret agent older brother. Schlesinger's film is not without its flaws – it takes rather too long to get started and is too fragmented – but it's a very classy package, and one particular scene involving dentistry (which was actually trimmed when preview audiences found it nausea-inducing) will leave a lasting impression and is definitely not for the faint-hearted. **TOM HUTCHINSON**

CAST

Dustin Hoffman *Babe Levy* • Laurence Olivier *Szell* • Roy Scheider *Doc Levy* • William Devane *Janeway* • Marthe Keller *Elsa* • Fritz Weaver *Professor Biesenthal* • Richard Bright *Karl* • Marc Lawrence *Erhard* • Allen Joseph *Babe's father*

DIRECTOR

John Schlesinger

SCREENPLAY

William Goldman, from his novel

DVD EXTRAS

Rehearsal footage; *Remembering Marathon Man* cast and crew interviews; *The Magic of Hollywood Is the Magic of People* featurette; trailer.

CONTENT ADVICE

Contains violence, a sex scene, swearing, nudity.

QUOTE UNQUOTE

Is it safe? **DR SZELL**

IF YOU ENJOYED THIS, WHY NOT TRY . . .

The Boys from Brazil (1978)
The Odessa File (1974)

DID YOU KNOW?

The character Dr Szell is based on the real-life Josef Mengele, the infamous SS medical officer at Auschwitz known as the "Angel of Death", who was on the run in South America when the movie was produced.

Memento

CERTIFICATE: **15** | YEAR: **2000** | COUNTRY: **US** | **COLOUR AND BW** | RUNNING TIME: **108 MINUTES**

SYNOPSIS

Leonard Shelby is determined to avenge the rape and murder of his wife, but is hampered by short-term memory loss following a head injury. Forced to record everything with copious notes, Polaroid photographs and even tattoos, Leonard's obsession leads him into a world where no-one can be trusted.

REVIEW

This dazzling, highly original "anti-thriller" has a complex, jumbled narrative that moves backwards in time. Thus we begin with the climactic murder then regress through the events that led up to it. Matters are complicated by the fact that the person investigating the killing (Guy Pearce) suffers from a rare form of amnesia, leaving him with no short-term memory. The mystery requires a lot of concentration, but the stunning final scene is ample reward. Not just an indulgence, the ingenious structure makes the point that memory, although unreliable, is what we depend upon for our sense of reality. The film brought the name of writer/director Christopher Nolan to the world's attention, and he fulfilled the promise shown here by going on to rejuvenate the Batman franchise with *Batman Begins* and *The Dark Knight*. **DAVID MCGILLIVRAY**

CAST

Guy Pearce *Leonard Shelby* • Carrie-Anne Moss *Natalie* • Joe Pantoliano *Teddy* • Mark Boone Junior *Burt* • Stephen Tobolowsky *Sammy Jankis* • Harriet Sansom Harris *Mrs Jankis* • Callum Keith Rennie *Dodd*

DIRECTOR

Christopher Nolan

SCREENPLAY

Christopher Nolan, from a short story by Jonathan Nolan

DVD EXTRAS

Three-disc Special Edition: commentary by Christopher Nolan; interviews with Christopher Nolan, Guy Pearce; biographies; three alternative endings; *Anatomy of a Scene* documentary; reverse version of film; split screen with shooting script; complete text of *Memento Mori* short story; stills and production sketches gallery; concept art gallery; poster gallery; web links; theatrical trailer.

CONTENT ADVICE

Contains violence, swearing.

QUOTE UNQUOTE

My wife deserves vengeance. It doesn't make a difference whether I know about it. Just because there are things I don't remember – doesn't make my actions meaningless.
LEONARD SHELBY

IF YOU ENJOYED THIS, WHY NOT TRY . . .

Déjà Vu (2006)
The Pledge (2000)

DID YOU KNOW?

The muscles that Australian star Guy Pearce shows off in *Memento* were first honed in his teens when he took up body building to bulk up his skinny frame. He went on to win the Junior Mr Victoria body-building competition when he was 15.

Misery

CERTIFICATE: **18** | YEAR: **1990** | COUNTRY: **US** | **COLOUR** | RUNNING TIME: **102 MINUTES**

SYNOPSIS

In a remote area of Colorado, successful novelist Paul Sheldon is injured in a car accident and taken in by ex-nurse Annie Wilkes, a devoted fan of Sheldon and his fictional heroine Misery Chastain. But events take a sinister turn when the novelist allows Wilkes to read a proof of his latest book.

REVIEW

This superb adaptation of Stephen King's bestseller from director Rob Reiner and screenwriter William Goldman deals with the trappings of celebrity, fanatical devotion, artistic dilemmas and the worthiness of commercial fiction within a psychological suspense context. Kathy Bates deservedly won a best actress Oscar for her monstrously scary performance as novelist James Caan's "Number One Fan". She changes from caring saviour and nurse to insane "Baby Jane" torturer after learning he's killed off her favourite literary character so he can turn his back on romantic potboilers to become a "serious" writer. While not a true-blue horror movie, Reiner's adept exercise in chilling claustrophobia nevertheless contains numerous jolts, with the sledgehammer "hobbling" scene certain to evoke screams of revulsion. **ALAN JONES**

CAST

James Caan *Paul Sheldon* • Kathy Bates *Annie Wilkes* • Richard Farnsworth *Buster, Sheriff* • Frances Sternhagen *Virginia* • Lauren Bacall *Marcia Sindell* • Graham Jarvis *Libby* • Jerry Potter *Pete*

DIRECTOR

Rob Reiner

SCREENPLAY

William Goldman, from the novel by Stephen King

AWARDS

Academy Awards (1): Actress (Kathy Bates)

DVD EXTRAS

Special Edition: commentary by Rob Reiner; commentary by William Goldman; *Misery Loves Company* documentary; *Mark Sharman's Musical Misery Tour* featurette; photo gallery; trailers.

CONTENT ADVICE

Contains violence, swearing.

QUOTE UNQUOTE

Now the time has come. I put two bullets in my gun. One for me, and one for you. Oh darling, it will be so beautiful.
ANNIE WILKES

IF YOU ENJOYED THIS, WHY NOT TRY . . .

The King of Comedy (1983)
Play Misty for Me (1971)

DID YOU KNOW?

Director Rob Reiner has a cameo as a helicopter pilot.

Mulholland Drive

CERTIFICATE: **15** | YEAR: **2001** | COUNTRY: **US/FR** | **COLOUR** | RUNNING TIME: **140 MINUTES**

SYNOPSIS

After an attempt on her life leaves her with amnesia, a beautiful woman stumbles into the apartment of Betty Elms, a fresh-faced Canadian just arrived in Hollywood. The mystery woman adopts the name Rita and together with Betty sets out to find who she is, a quest that will lead them to a dead body.

REVIEW

As twisted as the Los Angeles road it takes its name from, this is a typically weird and wonderful rumination on the American Dream, the Hollywood nightmare and the mysterious grey area in between from director David Lynch. Easily his most demanding work since *Fire Walk with Me*, Lynch's dazzling thriller reaches new heights of mesmeric fascination thanks to scintillating visuals and an offbeat emotional intensity. Although many plot strands are thrown into the suspenseful mix, the main focus is on the bizarre relationship between amnesiac movie star Laura Elena Harring and wannabe actress Naomi Watts. Unfolding like "The Anne Heche Story" as viewed through a kinky kaleidoscope, Lynch's surrealist fantasia does go over familiar territory – trademark dwarves, camp retro pop songs, symbolic imagery – but with a heightened edge of incisive observation. **ALAN JONES**

QUOTE UNQUOTE

It'll be just like in the movies – pretending to be somebody else. **BETTY ELMS**

IF YOU ENJOYED THIS, WHY NOT TRY . . .

The Hole (2001)
Rashomon (1950)

CAST

Naomi Watts *Betty Elms/Diane Selwyn* • Laura Elena Harring [Laura Harring] *Rita/Camilla Rhodes* • Justin Theroux *Adam Kesher* • Ann Miller *Coco Lenoix* • Dan Hedaya *Vincenzo Castigliane* • Mark Pellegrino *Joe* • Brent Briscoe *Detective Domgaard* • Robert Forster *Det Harry McKnight* • Lee Grant *Louise Bonner* • Michael J Anderson *Mr Rocque* • Billy Ray Cyrus *Gene* • Chad Everett *Jimmy Katz* • Angelo Badalamenti *Luigi Castigliane*

DIRECTOR

David Lynch

SCREENPLAY

David Lynch

AWARDS

Baftas (1): Editing

DVD EXTRAS

Two-disc Special Edition: making-of documentary; Cannes press conference; interviews with David Lynch, Naomi Watts, Justin Theroux, Laura Harring, Mary Sweeney, Angelo Badalamenti; preview of *Inland Empire*; booklet containing extract from Faber & Faber's *Lynch on Lynch*; theatrical trailer.

DID YOU KNOW?

David Lynch made this as an $8 million pilot episode in an unsuccessful attempt to turn it into a TV series. But French company StudioCanal and some of the movie's producers put up another $7 million, allowing Lynch to complete the film.

The Night of the Hunter

CERTIFICATE: **12** | YEAR: **1955** | COUNTRY: **US** | **BW** | RUNNING TIME: **88 MINUTES**

SYNOPSIS

Shortly before his arrest for murder, Ben Harper tells his son John where he has hidden a large sum of stolen money. After Harper is hanged, John and his sister Pearl receive a visit from their father's ex-cellmate, a sinister preacher with "love" and "hate" tattooed on the knuckles of his hands.

REVIEW

This thriller is one of the great masterpieces of American cinema, a movie so strangely repellent, so poetic and so hypnotic that it sadly never found an audience. It was Charles Laughton's only film as director, and it features Robert Mitchum's finest screen performance as a bogus priest and psychopath who has "love" and "hate" tattooed on his hands. Serving time in jail, Mitchum learns about a bank robbery from a condemned man, and on his release he pursues the man's children in the belief they can lead him to a cache of stolen money. Mitchum's menacing presence is heightened by Laughton to an extraordinary degree, and their stunning collaboration is enhanced by Lillian Gish's portrayal of a gun-toting spinster. Set during the Depression in a rural backwater where the riverbanks are alive with croaking frogs, it's a fairy tale turned into a dark night of the soul. **ADRIAN TURNER**

QUOTE UNQUOTE

These fingers, dear hearts, is always a-warrin' and a-tuggin', one agin the other. **HARRY POWELL**

IF YOU ENJOYED THIS, WHY NOT TRY . . .

The Golden Compass (2007)
Something Wicked This Way Comes (1983) ■

CAST

Robert Mitchum *Preacher Harry Powell* • Shelley Winters *Willa Harper* • Lillian Gish *Rachel* • Evelyn Varden *Icey Spoon* • Peter Graves *Ben Harper* • Billy Chapin *John* • Sally Jane Bruce *Pearl* • James Gleason *Birdie*

DIRECTOR

Charles Laughton

SCREENPLAY

James Agee, from the novel by Davis Grubb

DVD EXTRAS

Theatrical trailer.

DID YOU KNOW?

The character Harry Powell was inspired by real-life murderer Harry Powers, who was hanged in 1932.

Nikita

CERTIFICATE: **18** | YEAR: **1990** | COUNTRY: **FR/IT** | **COLOUR** | RUNNING TIME: **112 MINUTES**

SYNOPSIS

Nikita, a violent drug-addicted girl, takes part in a drugstore robbery that ends in carnage. She is given a choice: death row or being trained as a government secret service agent and assassin. Nikita proves an apt pupil, but complications arise on the outside when she falls for an ordinary guy.

REVIEW

After being involved in a robbery, vicious junkie Anne Parillaud is reprogrammed as an assassin for a secret government agency in this extremely exciting thriller with a feminist slant from French director Luc Besson. In paying homage to American action movies, Besson goes one better than his clear inspirations, to craft a beautifully stylised, enthralling and very violent comic strip. Parillaud (married to Besson at the time) is tremendous as the unscrupulous hit woman and Jeanne Moreau's charm teacher cameo is a gem. But it's Besson's boldly modern approach to traditional *film noir* material that makes this elemental mind-blower so striking. It proved so successful that it was remade in 1993 by John Badham as *Point of No Return* (aka *The Assassin*) starring Bridget Fonda, which then spawned a long-running TV series. **ALAN JONES**

CAST

Anne Parillaud *Nikita* • Jean-Hugues Anglade *Marco* • Tcheky Karyo *Bob* • Jeanne Moreau *Amande* • Jean Reno *Victor the cleaner* • Marc Duret *Rico* • Philippe Leroy-Beaulieu *Grossman*

DIRECTOR

Luc Besson

SCREENPLAY

Luc Besson

DVD EXTRAS

New Luc Besson Collection version released September 2009. No details available. Also available on Blu-ray.

CONTENT ADVICE

Contains violence, swearing.

QUOTE UNQUOTE

Mister, is this heaven here or not? **NIKITA**

IF YOU ENJOYED THIS, WHY NOT TRY . . .

The Assassin (1993)
The Long Kiss Goodnight (1996)

DID YOU KNOW?

Growing up on the Mediterranean coast with his diving instructor parents, it's no surprise that Luc Besson wanted to be a marine biologist when he was younger. But an accident at 17 meant that he had to give up diving for a time.

North by Northwest

CERTIFICATE: **PG** | YEAR: **1959** | COUNTRY: **US** | **COLOUR** | RUNNING TIME: **130 MINUTES**

SYNOPSIS

Advertising executive Roger Thornhill is put in deadly peril when he is mistaken for the mysterious "Mr Kaplan" by a ruthless espionage organisation. Failing to convince them of his identity, Thornhill tracks down the one man who can prove his story only to find himself accused of murder.

REVIEW

This Hitchcock classic contains extra-generous helpings of the ingredients that make his films so unmissable. Action, intrigue, romance and comedy are blended throughout with consummate skill; the attack by the crop-dusting plane and the finale on Mount Rushmore are simply the icing on the cake. Rarely did Hitchcock have as much fun with his favourite "innocent in peril" theme or make such inventive use of famous landmarks. In his fourth and final collaboration with the "Master of Suspense", Cary Grant is the personification of suaveness as a hapless Manhattan advertising executive who is forced to take on a nest of enemy agents, led by a rather disengaged James Mason. Add in Saul Bass's simple yet memorable title sequence and Bernard Herrmann's suspenseful score, and you have one of the best of Hitchcock's Hollywood thrillers. **DAVID PARKINSON**

CAST

Cary Grant *Roger Thornhill* • Eva Marie Saint *Eve Kendall* • James Mason *Phillip Vandamm* • Jessie Royce Landis *Clara Thornhill* • Leo G Carroll *Professor* • Philip Ober *Lester Townsend* • Martin Landau *Leonard* • Adam Williams *Valerian*

DIRECTOR

Alfred Hitchcock

SCREENPLAY

Ernest Lehman

DVD EXTRAS

Destination Hitchcock: the Making of North by Northwest documentary hosted by Eva Marie Saint; commentary by screenwriter Ernest Lehman; music only track featuring Bernard Herrmann's score; TV spot; trailer; stills gallery.

QUOTE UNQUOTE

The moment I meet an attractive woman, I have to start pretending I have no desire to make love to her.
ROGER THORNHILL

IF YOU ENJOYED THIS, WHY NOT TRY . . .

The Fugitive (1993)
Saboteur (1942)

DID YOU KNOW?

According to Alfred Hitchcock, one of the film's discarded titles was "The Man on Lincoln's Nose". However, officials from Mount Rushmore insisted that Hitch drop a sequence in which Cary Grant slides down Abe's nose, so the title couldn't be used.

Notorious

CERTIFICATE: **U** | YEAR: **1946** | COUNTRY: **US** | **BW** | RUNNING TIME: **100 MINUTES**

SYNOPSIS

The daughter of a Nazi sympathiser, Alicia Huberman gets the chance to prove her loyalty to the US by infiltrating a Nazi spy ring in Rio. Her American contact begins to fall for her, and is outraged when he finds out Alicia's mission is to seduce scientist Alexander Sebastian, a friend of her father.

REVIEW

Scripted by hard-boiled veteran Ben Hecht, this dark romantic thriller isn't as thematically complex or technically audacious as some of Alfred Hitchcock's later classics, but it's still hard to beat for pure, polished entertainment. Cary Grant and Ingrid Bergman are perfectly paired as an American agent and the high-living daughter of a Nazi sympathiser whom he has under surveillance. Yet they're almost upstaged by Claude Rains, who manages to invest his treacherous villain with a modicum of humanity. This contrasts strikingly with Grant's surface steel, as he nonchalantly places the woman he loves (Bergman) in danger by persuading her to marry Rains to secure some inside information. Hitch permits himself one moment of visual virtuosity (a stunning crane shot swooping towards a key in Bergman's hand), but mostly confines himself to spinning his yarn with customarily mischievous skill. **DAVID PARKINSON**

QUOTE UNQUOTE

I want to make it 80 and wipe that grin off your face. I don't like gentlemen who grin at me. **ALICIA HUBERMAN**

IF YOU ENJOYED THIS, WHY NOT TRY . . .

Betrayed (1988)
Mission: Impossible 2 (1999)

CAST

Cary Grant *TR Devlin* • Ingrid Bergman *Alicia Huberman* • Claude Rains *Alexander Sebastian* • Louis Calhern *Paul Prescott* • Madame Konstantin [Leopoldine Konstantin] *Mme Anna Sebastian* • Reinhold Schünzel *Dr Anderson/Otto Rensler*

DIRECTOR

Alfred Hitchcock

SCREENPLAY

Ben Hecht

DVD EXTRAS

A conversation with Hitchcock; interview with film critic and writer Kim Newman; Hitchcock biography; quotes and trivia; cast biographies; photo gallery; awards and taglines.

DID YOU KNOW?

Alfred Hitchcock claimed he was under surveillance by the FBI because the plot involved uranium.

Oldboy

CERTIFICATE: **18** | YEAR: **2003** | COUNTRY: **S KOR** | **COLOUR** | RUNNING TIME: **114 MINUTES**

SYNOPSIS

Oh Dae-su is kidnapped and imprisoned for no apparent reason. He is then horrified to discover that his wife has been murdered and he is the chief suspect. After being held for 15 years, his mind disorientated by hypnosis, he is released without explanation and sets about seeking vengeance.

REVIEW

Director Park Chan-wook demonstrated that his critically acclaimed *Sympathy for Mr Vengeance* was no flash in the pan when he received the Grand Prix at 2004's Cannes film festival for this mind-bending film. Choi Min-sik plays a happily married father who is kidnapped and incarcerated for no apparent reason. He then discovers that his wife has been murdered and he's the principal suspect. Fifteen years of unexplained detention follow. Suddenly, he wakes up to find himself free and gets down to the serious business of vengeance, leaving a trail of blood and mayhem that would make Quentin Tarantino proud. Some viewers will be repulsed by scenes of self-mutilation and the most painful visit to the dentist since *Marathon Man*, but this has more to offer than action and violence – it's an imaginative tale of guilt and revenge, with a shocking twist in the tale.

BRIAN PENDREIGH

CAST

Choi Min-sik *Oh Dae-su* • Yu Ji-tae *Lee Woo-jin* • Gang Hye-jung *Mido* • Chi Dae-han *No Joo-hwan* • Oh Dal-su *Park Cheol-woong* • Kim Byeong-ok *Chief guard (Mr Han)*

DIRECTOR

Park Chan-wook

SCREENPLAY

Hwang Jo-yun, Lim Joon-hyung, Park Chan-wook, from a story by Garon Tsuchiya, Nobuaki Minegishi

DVD EXTRAS

Commentary by Park Chan-wook; director's and cinematographer's commentary; director and cast commentary; theatrical trailer. Also available on Blu-ray.

CONTENT ADVICE

Contains violence.

QUOTE UNQUOTE
Revenge is good for your health. OH DAE-SU

IF YOU ENJOYED THIS, WHY NOT TRY . . .
The Count of Monte Cristo (1934)
Frantic (1988)

DID YOU KNOW?
South Korean actor Choi Min-sik needed four takes to perfect the scene in which he eats a live octopus in a sushi bar. Director Park Chan-wook explained: "He is a Buddhist, so before every take he would pray to the octopus, offering it his apology."

As American as apple pie.

Paramount Pictures Presents
AN ALAN J. PAKULA PRODUCTION
WARREN BEATTY
THE PARALLAX VIEW

Co-starring
HUME CRONYN · WILLIAM DANIELS and PAULA PRENTISS
Director of Photography GORDON WILLIS · Music Scored by MICHAEL SMALL
Executive Producer GABRIEL KATZKA · Screenplay by DAVID GILER and LORENZO SEMPLE, Jr.
Produced and Directed by ALAN J. PAKULA · PANAVISION® TECHNICOLOR® A Paramount Picture

The Parallax View

CERTIFICATE: **15** | YEAR: **1974** | COUNTRY: **US** | **COLOUR** | RUNNING TIME: **97 MINUTES**

SYNOPSIS

Journalist Joe Frady is among the witnesses to a political assassination at a rally in Seattle. Three years later he discovers that many of those who saw the killing have died suspiciously. Knowing he could be next, Frady sets out to uncover the truth and is led to the sinister Parallax organisation.

REVIEW

Two years before he directed the Oscar-winning *All the President's Men*, Alan J Pakula made this equally potent and startlingly similar conspiracy thriller. Investigating a political assassination that he witnessed three years earlier, reporter Warren Beatty uncovers evidence of a sinister agency called the Parallax Corporation, which recruits its marksmen from the dregs of disillusioned society. He also discovers that other witnesses to the assassination are being bumped off and that his life is in danger. With an excellent script by David Giler and Lorenzo Semple Jr, stunning photography by *The Godfather* cameraman Gordon Willis, and perfect acting (William Daniels and Hume Cronyn are among the supporting players), the story of Beatty's infiltration of the society and his attempt to foil yet another killing is riveting, fascinating and nerve-racking by turn.

ALAN JONES

CAST

Warren Beatty *Joe Frady* • Paula Prentiss *Lee Carter* • William Daniels *Austin Tucker* • Walter McGinn *Jack Younger* • Hume Cronyn *Rintels* • Kelly Thordsen *LD* • Chuck Waters *Assassin* • Earl Hindman *Red*

DIRECTOR

Alan J Pakula

SCREENPLAY

David Giler, Lorenzo Semple Jr, from the novel by Loren Singer

DVD EXTRAS

Original theatrical trailer.

CONTENT ADVICE

Contains violence, swearing.

QUOTE UNQUOTE

I'm dead, Bill. I just want to stay that way for a while.

JOE FRADY

IF YOU ENJOYED THIS, WHY NOT TRY . . .

The Manchurian Candidate (1962)
Three Days of the Condor (1975)

■

DID YOU KNOW?

Only six years after the 1968 assassination of presidential candidate Robert F Kennedy, this film's opening was set up to echo the events of that day.

Peeping Tom

CERTIFICATE: **15** | YEAR: **1960** | COUNTRY: **UK** | **COLOUR** | RUNNING TIME: **97 MINUTES**

SYNOPSIS

A disturbed film technician becomes obsessed by expressions of fear after being subjected to experiments on the nervous system by his scientist father when he was a boy. Armed with a deadly camera, he perfects a method of capturing the final facial contortions of female visitors to his studio.

REVIEW

This infamous thriller was director Michael Powell's first solo project after 20 years of collaboration with Emeric Pressburger. A Freudian nightmare about a film technician (Carl Boehm) who photographs the look of terror in the eyes of the women he kills, it was badly received at the time by British critics who were offended by the sexual and violent images, and it destroyed Powell's reputation in this country. Only in recent years has *Peeping Tom* been recognised, by directors such as Martin Scorsese (who was instrumental in having the film restored and re-released in the late-1970s), as a risk-all masterpiece from one of our greatest film-makers. Maxine Audley and Moira Shearer are among those who encounter the killer's lethal voyeurism, while Powell casts his own son, Columba, as the lad who would grow up to kill and himself as the father who created a monster. **TOM HUTCHINSON**

QUOTE UNQUOTE

Whatever I photograph, I always lose. **MARK LEWIS**

IF YOU ENJOYED THIS, WHY NOT TRY . . .

M (1931)
Psycho (1960)

CAST

Carl Boehm [Karlheinz Böhm] *Mark Lewis* • Moira Shearer *Vivian* • Anna Massey *Helen Stephens* • Maxine Audley *Mrs Stephens* • Esmond Knight *Arthur Baden* • Bartlett Mullins *Mr Peters* • Shirley Anne Field *Diane Ashley* • Michael Goodliffe *Don Jarvis* • Brenda Bruce *Dora*

DIRECTOR

Michael Powell

SCREENPLAY

Leo Marks

DVD EXTRAS

Special Edition: introduction by Martin Scorsese; commentary by Michael Powell expert Ian Christie; interview with Thelma Schoonmaker (Oscar-winning editor and Michael Powell's widow); *The Eye of the Beholder* documentary; *The Strange Gaze of Mark Lewis* documentary; behind-the-scenes stills gallery; booklet featuring an interview with screenwriter Leo Marks and an extract from Michael Powell's autobiography.

DID YOU KNOW?

One of the cameras in Carl Boehm's room is a hand-operated Bell & Howell Eyemo that director Michael Powell won in a competition as a young man.

Play Misty for Me

CERTIFICATE: **18** | YEAR: **1971** | COUNTRY: **US** | **COLOUR** | RUNNING TIME: **97 MINUTES**

SYNOPSIS

Dave Garver, an all-night DJ at a small radio station in California, has a fling with a woman he meets in a bar. She turns out to be the persistent female fan who repeatedly requests the song *Misty* on his show and her obsessive nature soon begins to take a toll on his life.

REVIEW

Clint Eastwood made the first step towards establishing himself as a top talent behind the camera – and winning best director Oscars for *Unforgiven* (1992) and *Million Dollar Baby* (2004) – with this fine thriller, in which he also stars. Eastwood is totally convincing as a DJ who rejects an avid fan (Jessica Walter) after a one-night stand only to discover that she's determined to keep him whatever the cost – and all this 16 years before *Fatal Attraction*. Jealousy is one of the hardest emotions to portray with any kind of subtlety in cinema, yet Walter is superb as the deranged woman. Eastwood's sideburns and flares lend the movie a period charm today, but its power to grip and chill remains undiminished. Look out for *Dirty Harry* director Don Siegel (Eastwood's mentor) as Murphy the bartender, and don't watch this one on your own. **TONY SLOMAN**

QUOTE UNQUOTE

You ever find yourself getting completely smothered by someone? **DAVE GARVER**

IF YOU ENJOYED THIS, WHY NOT TRY . . .

Fatal Attraction (1987)
The Hand That Rocks the Cradle (1992)

CAST

Clint Eastwood *Dave Garver* • Jessica Walter *Evelyn Draper* • Donna Mills *Tobie Williams* • John Larch *Sergeant McCallum* • James McEachin *Al Monte* • Donald Siegel [Don Siegel] *Murphy the bartender*

DIRECTOR

Clint Eastwood

SCREENPLAY

Jo Heims, Dean Riesner, from a story by Heims

DVD EXTRAS

30th Anniversary Edition: *Play It Again* a look back at *Play Misty for Me*; *The Beguiled, Misty, Don and Clint* with film historian Richard Schickel; photo montage: Clint Eastwood acts and directs, evolution of a poster; Clint Eastwood on DVD; cast and film-maker biographies; production notes; theatrical trailer; DVD rom with extra features.

CONTENT ADVICE

Contains swearing, drug abuse, brief nudity.

DID YOU KNOW?

The film is set in Carmel, California, where Clint Eastwood became mayor in 1986.

There are two kinds
of people in his
up-tight world:
his victims
and his women.
And sometimes
you can't tell
them apart.

Metro-Goldwyn-Mayer presents
A Judd Bernard-Irwin Winkler
Production

LEE MARVIN
"POINT BLANK"

co-starring
ANGIE DICKINSON · KEENAN WYNN · CARROLL O'CONNOR · LLOYD BOCHNER · MICHAEL STRONG [Suggested For Mature Audiences]
Screenplay by Alexander Jacobs and David Newhouse & Rafe Newhouse · Based on the Novel The Hunter by Richard Stark · Directed by John Boorman · Produced by Judd Bernard and Robert Chartoff
In Panavision® and Metrocolor
MGM

Point Blank

CERTIFICATE: **18** | YEAR: **1967** | COUNTRY: **US** | **COLOUR** | RUNNING TIME: **87 MINUTES**

SYNOPSIS

After stealing a fortune in loot from a rival gang in the deserted prison at Alcatraz, a man called Walker is shot and left for dead by his partner in crime while his conniving wife looks on. Miraculously surviving the attack, Walker sets out to seek revenge and retrieve his share of the money.

REVIEW

This grim, violent thriller marked the US directing debut of John Boorman (he'd previously made a Dave Clark Five musical in Britain). It's a gripping, sexy action movie, with a magnificent performance from Lee Marvin as the revenge-seeking Walker, whose insane quest to retrieve Mob money assumes mythical proportions. Based on a novel by Richard Stark (the pseudonym of Donald E Westlake), it's a markedly superior work, with wonderful cinematography by Philip H Lathrop that makes the most of impressive Los Angeles night locations and subtly complex storytelling. Marvin is perfectly cast as the seemingly indestructible loner and he's brilliantly supported by Angie Dickinson as his reluctant partner in retribution. Incredible as it seems, MGM executives were so worried by the rushes that it took an intervention from David Lean to ensure Boorman remained on the picture. **ADRIAN TURNER**

CAST

Lee Marvin *Walker* • Angie Dickinson *Chris* • Keenan Wynn *Yost* • Carroll O'Connor *Brewster* • Lloyd Bochner *Frederick Carter* • Michael Strong *Stegman* • John Vernon *Mal Reese* • Sharon Acker *Lynne* • James Sikking [James B Sikking] *Hired gun*

DIRECTOR

John Boorman

SCREENPLAY

Alexander Jacobs, David Newhouse, Rafe Newhouse, from the novel *The Hunter* by Richard Stark [Donald E Westlake]

CONTENT ADVICE

Contains violence, swearing.

QUOTE UNQUOTE

Somebody's got to pay. **WALKER**

IF YOU ENJOYED THIS, WHY NOT TRY ...

Payback (1997)

DID YOU KNOW?

This was the first major production to film on Alcatraz after the prison closed in 1963.

Point Break

CERTIFICATE: **18** | YEAR: **1991** | COUNTRY: **US** | **COLOUR** | RUNNING TIME: **122 MINUTES**

SYNOPSIS

Novice FBI agent Johnny Utah is assigned with veteran partner Angelo Pappas to track down a gang of bank robbers who carry out their raids wearing masks of former American presidents. In the belief that the gang are surfers, Utah goes undercover to learn surfing skills and meets the enigmatic Bodhi.

REVIEW

Following the exciting Jamie Lee Curtis vehicle *Blue Steel*, director Kathryn Bigelow cemented her action credentials with this silly but hugely enjoyable thriller. Keanu Reeves plays the young FBI agent and, unsurprisingly, makes a very convincing surfing dude when he goes under cover to infiltrate a gang headed by twisted mystic Patrick Swayze (whose character, Bodhi, is named after the Buddhist term for enlightenment). Try to ignore the mystical claptrap and surf-talk, and concentrate instead on Bigelow's stunningly conceived action set pieces, as well as some exhilarating skydiving (Swayze did over 50 jumps himself) and surfing scenes. For Reeves, this proved to be a dry, or more accurately wet, run for *Speed*, and he acquits himself well, while Swayze makes a convincing enough villain, and, in support, Gary Busey provides some welcome grit as Reeves's partner. **JOHN FERGUSON**

QUOTE UNQUOTE

If you want the ultimate, you've got to be willing to pay the ultimate price. It's not tragic to die doing what you love. **BODHI**

IF YOU ENJOYED THIS, WHY NOT TRY . . .

Big Wednesday (1978)
Drop Zone (1994)

CAST

Patrick Swayze *Bodhi* • Keanu Reeves *Johnny Utah* • Gary Busey *Angelo Pappas* • Lori Petty *Tyler* • John C McGinley *Ben Harp* • James LeGros *Roach* • John Philbin *Nathanial*

DIRECTOR

Kathryn Bigelow

SCREENPLAY

W Peter Iliff, from a story by Rick King, Iliff

DVD EXTRAS

Original theatrical trailer.

CONTENT ADVICE

Contains violence, swearing, nudity.

DID YOU KNOW?

Twelve years after the movie, *Point Break Live!* hit the stage in America. The production claimed to capture the raw energy of Keanu Reeves in the movie by selecting a member of each audience to play Johnny Utah using cue cards.

The Postman Always Rings Twice

CERTIFICATE: **PG** | YEAR: **1946** | COUNTRY: **US** | **BW** | RUNNING TIME: **108 MINUTES**

SYNOPSIS

Drifter Frank Chambers takes a job as a handyman at a roadside café where he begins a torrid affair with the owner's beautiful young wife, Cora. She's bored with her dead-end life and her oafish, older husband and soon the lovers' uncontrollable passion prompts thoughts of murder.

REVIEW

Sweaty and sensuous, this MGM *film noir* remains utterly electrifying today thanks to the riveting sexual chemistry between its stars, Lana Turner and John Garfield, and Tay Garnett's tense directorial style. Garnett clearly understood the world of James M Cain's original novel, though he was forced to circumvent certain sections because of the censorship demands of the day. Despite competition from several other movies, notably Luchino Visconti's *Ossessione* and Bob Rafelson's 1981 film starring Jack Nicholson and Jessica Lange, this has proved to be the definitive interpretation of the novel. There's a powerful supporting cast (the benign Cecil Kellaway as Turner's cuckolded husband and Hume Cronyn as a conniving lawyer). But it's the Turner/Garfield coupling that's at the incandescent heart of this film – their first meeting remains a classic moment of screen desire. **TONY SLOMAN**

CAST
Lana Turner *Cora Smith* • John Garfield *Frank Chambers* • Cecil Kellaway *Nick Smith* • Hume Cronyn *Arthur Keats* • Leon Ames *Kyle Sackett* • Audrey Totter *Madge Gorland*

DIRECTOR
Tay Garnett

SCREENPLAY
Harry Ruskin, Niven Busch, from the novel by James M Cain

DVD EXTRAS
Introduction by film historian and author Richard Jewel; documentary *The John Garfield Story*; theatrical trailer.

QUOTE UNQUOTE

With my brains and your looks, we could go places.
FRANK CHAMBERS

IF YOU ENJOYED THIS, WHY NOT TRY ...
Ossessione (1942)
The Postman Always Rings Twice (1981)

DID YOU KNOW?
The film-makers were worried about getting the racier content past the censors, so they dressed Lana Turner in white. Director Tay Garnett said: "We figured that... somehow made everything she did less sensuous. It was also attractive as hell."

Psycho

CERTIFICATE: **15** | YEAR: **1960** | COUNTRY: **US** | **BW** | RUNNING TIME: **108 MINUTES**

SYNOPSIS

Impulsively absconding with $40,000 of her employer's money, Marion Crane sets off to join her lover in California. Plagued by fear and regret, she endures a tiring drive in the rain, finally stopping at a lonely motel run by Norman Bates, an intense young man who lives with his domineering mother.

REVIEW

Notorious for its hugely influential shower scene, this is easily the most shocking film produced by the "Master of Suspense". Yet Alfred Hitchcock always maintained that it was actually a black comedy. Working with a TV crew, he completed the picture for a mere $800,000. But the California Gothic tale of the sinister goings-on at the Bates Motel went on to become his biggest commercial success. The opening segment, involving Janet Leigh and an envelope of stolen cash, is the biggest "MacGuffin" in Hitchcock's career. His most audacious achievement, however, was in getting us to side with creepy motel proprietor Norman Bates against the authorities, Leigh's lover and sister, and Bates's incessantly shrewish mother. Three sequels and Gus Van Sant's pointless 1998 scene-by-scene colour remake followed, but none even came close to this memorable masterpiece. **DAVID PARKINSON**

CAST

Anthony Perkins *Norman Bates* • Janet Leigh *Marion Crane* • Vera Miles *Lila Crane* • John Gavin *Sam Loomis* • Martin Balsam *Milton Arbogast* • John McIntire *Sheriff Chambers* • Simon Oakland *Dr Richmond*

DIRECTOR

Alfred Hitchcock

SCREENPLAY

Joseph Stefano, from the novel by Robert Bloch

DVD EXTRAS

45th Anniversary Special Edition: *The Hitchcock Legacy* including an interview with Hitchcock. The original DVD release has production notes and original theatrical trailer.

QUOTE UNQUOTE

A boy's best friend is his mother. **NORMAN BATES**

IF YOU ENJOYED THIS, WHY NOT TRY . . .

Les Diaboliques (1954)
The Shining (1980)

DID YOU KNOW?

The film is based on the pulp novel by Robert Bloch, and after Alfred Hitchcock acquired the movie rights he tried to keep the ending a surprise by taking as many copies as possible of the book off the market.

Alfred Hitchcock
The Master of **Suspense**

brings you
his masterpiece!

They stared too long... saw too much!

PARAMOUNT presents **James Stewart**

in

Alfred Hitchcock's

Rear Window

co-starring

GRACE KELLY · WENDELL COREY · THELMA RITTER

with **RAYMOND BURR**

COLOR BY
TECHNICOLOR

DIRECTED BY
ALFRED HITCHCOCK · SCREENPLAY BY JOHN MICHAEL HAYES · BASED ON THE SHORT STORY BY CORNELL WOOLRICH

Rear Window

CERTIFICATE: **PG** | YEAR: **1954** | COUNTRY: **US** | **COLOUR** | RUNNING TIME: **109 MINUTES**

SYNOPSIS

Confined to a wheelchair following an accident, photographer Jeff Jeffries passes the time observing his neighbours. He becomes intrigued by a man who he sees leaving his flat one night with a suitcase, and whose wife has seemingly disappeared. So Jeff and his girlfriend Lisa decide to investigate.

REVIEW

Like his earlier (but less successful) *Rope*, this masterpiece from director Alfred Hitchcock began as a technical stunt: Hitchcock wondered if he could make a film on just a single set and from just one vantage point. His *Rope* star James Stewart was also back on board to play the photojournalist who whiles away the time gazing out of the window and becomes convinced that a neighbour opposite (Raymond Burr) has murdered his wife. Hitchcock's "stunt" became a classic study of voyeurism – all those windows, shaped like movie screens, each containing a mini-drama of its own – and the tension builds brilliantly, complemented perfectly by the sexy repartee between the immobile Stewart and the slinky Grace Kelly, and the dry, cynical humour provided by Thelma Ritter as Stewart's nurse. Often imitated, this extraordinary achievement has never been equalled. **ADRIAN TURNER**

QUOTE UNQUOTE

I've seen it through that window. I've seen bickering and family quarrels and mysterious trips at night, knives and saws and ropes, and now since last evening, not a sign of the wife. **LB "JEFF" JEFFRIES**

IF YOU ENJOYED THIS, WHY NOT TRY ...

Body Double (1984)
Disturbia (2007)

CAST

James Stewart *LB "Jeff" Jeffries* • Grace Kelly *Lisa Carol Fremont* • Wendell Corey *Detective Thomas J Doyle* • Thelma Ritter *Stella* • Raymond Burr *Lars Thorwald* • Judith Evelyn *Miss Lonely Hearts* • David Seville [Ross Bagdasarian] *Songwriter* • Georgine Darcy *Miss Torso* • Sara Berner *Woman on fire escape*

DIRECTOR

Alfred Hitchcock

SCREENPLAY

John Michael Hayes, from the short story *It Had to Be Murder* by Cornell Woolrich

DVD EXTRAS

Documentary: *Rear Window Ethics: Remembering and Restoring a Hitchcock Classic*; making-of featurette with screenwriter John Michael Hayes; compilation of Hitchcock trailers introduced by James Stewart; original theatrical trailer; art gallery.

DID YOU KNOW?

Alfred Hitchcock's hatred of Hollywood producer David O Selznick was so intense by the time he made *Rear Window* that he had Raymond Burr, who played the murder suspect, made up to look like the movie mogul.

Rebecca

CERTIFICATE: **PG** | YEAR: **1940** | COUNTRY: **US** | **BW** | RUNNING TIME: **125 MINUTES**

SYNOPSIS

Wealthy widower Maxim de Winter returns from Monte Carlo to his family estate in Cornwall, bringing with him his timid young bride. But the second Mrs de Winter soon finds herself haunted by the spirit of her husband's beautiful first wife, Rebecca, who died in mysterious circumstances.

REVIEW

Alfred Hitchcock's first Hollywood film is a sumptuous and suspenseful adaptation of Daphne du Maurier's romantic novel. Produced by David O Selznick, it is immaculately played and was rightly awarded the Oscar for best picture. That Laurence Olivier as Maxim de Winter is superb goes without saying, but it's mousey Joan Fontaine who is a revelation as the second Mrs de Winter – if Olivier had got his way, it would have been his future wife Vivien Leigh in the role, but Selznick overruled him. Lovers of lesbian subtexts will have a field day with Judith Anderson's sinister housekeeper Mrs Danvers, as Hitchcock circumvents the Hays Code censors who forced him to make changes to the original story. Fortunately no damage was done – unless you think too hard. And, since the style and pace never let up, there's no danger of that. **TONY SLOMAN**

QUOTE UNQUOTE

Last night, I dreamt I went to Manderley again.
MRS DE WINTER

IF YOU ENJOYED THIS, WHY NOT TRY . . .
My Cousin Rachel (1952)

CAST

Laurence Olivier *Maxim de Winter* • Joan Fontaine *Mrs de Winter* • George Sanders *Jack Favell* • Judith Anderson *Mrs Danvers* • Nigel Bruce *Major Giles Lacy* • Reginald Denny *Frank Crawley* • C Aubrey Smith *Colonel Julyan* • Gladys Cooper *Beatrice Lacy* • Florence Bates *Mrs Edythe Van Hopper* • Melville Cooper *Coroner* • Leo G Carroll *Dr Baker* • Leonard Carey *Ben*

DIRECTOR

Alfred Hitchcock

SCREENPLAY

Robert E Sherwood, Joan Harrison, Philip MacDonald, Michael Hogan, Barbara Keon, from the novel by Daphne du Maurier

AWARDS

Academy Awards (2): Film, Cinematography (black and white)

DVD EXTRAS

Interview with Alfred Hitchcock; interview with film journalist Kim Newman; biographies of Laurence Olivier and Joan Fontaine; Hitchcock biography, quotes and trivia; biography of producer David O Selznick; production notes; slide show; François Truffaut on Hitchcock (text only).

DID YOU KNOW?

Hitchcock insisted that the film was shot in black and white to maintain the brooding atmosphere of the source novel.

Repulsion

CERTIFICATE: **18** | YEAR: **1965** | COUNTRY: **UK** | **BW** | RUNNING TIME: **100 MINUTES**

SYNOPSIS

Carol Ledoux is a repressed Belgian manicurist working in a small London salon. She shares a flat with her liberal sister, whose boyfriend occasionally visits. When the lovers go on holiday, Carol is left alone to give free rein to her fantasies and fears, and becomes dangerously unbalanced.

REVIEW

Director Roman Polanski takes us on a deeply disturbing, hallucinatory trip into Catherine Deneuve's mental breakdown in this claustrophobic British psychological thriller, his first film in English. As Swinging London parties in the background, repressed Belgian manicurist Deneuve unsheathes her claws with deadly results. There are shades of Buñuel and Cocteau, but Polanski puts his personal stamp on the violent visuals (the killing of a boyfriend and landlord, Deneuve's rape by an unknown assailant) and the terrifying soundtrack (the buzzing of flies, a slashing knife, the ticking of a clock). And all the while the viewer is left wondering what is real and where fantasy begins. The final panning shot revealing a photograph of Deneuve as a young girl, even then withdrawn and apart, is a truly cathartic moment. **TOM HUTCHINSON**

CAST

Catherine Deneuve *Carol Ledoux* • Ian Hendry *Michael* • John Fraser *Colin* • Patrick Wymark *Landlord* • Yvonne Furneaux *Helen Ledoux* • Renee Houston *Miss Balch* • Roman Polanski *Spoons player*

DIRECTOR

Roman Polanski

SCREENPLAY

Roman Polanski, Gérard Brach, David Stone

DVD EXTRAS

Commentary by Roman Polanski and Catherine Deneuve; documentary *A British Horror Film*; audio interview with Richard L Gregory, professor of neuro psychology at Bristol University; stills and production sketch gallery; cast and crew biographies; theatrical trailer.

CONTENT ADVICE

Contains violence.

QUOTE UNQUOTE

I must get this crack mended. **CAROL LEDOUX**

IF YOU ENJOYED THIS, WHY NOT TRY . . .

The Machinist (2003)
Persona (1966)

DID YOU KNOW?

Director Roman Polanski had to work with a limited budget while making this, his first feature after leaving Poland. Consequently, he made all the blood from cochineal (a crimson substance made from crushed insects of the same name) and instant coffee.

Le Samouraï

CERTIFICATE: **PG** | YEAR: **1967** | COUNTRY: **FR/IT** | **COLOUR** | RUNNING TIME: **100 MINUTES**

SYNOPSIS

A contract killer commits a murder, unperturbed by the presence of witnesses – the police question but are forced to release him as no-one comes forward. But news of his arrest gets out and soon he is on the run from the unknown man who commissioned his services, and from a dogged cop.

REVIEW

The then-32-year-old Alain Delon excels in this ultra-stylish study of the ultimate professional, playing ruthless, poker-faced assassin-for-hire Jeff Costello. The way in which director Jean-Pierre Melville sets up hitman Costello's next job is mesmerising, attending to each part of the preparation with the detailed eye of a true craftsman. Yet, as in every good *film noir*, there is a *femme fatale* waiting in the shadows to tempt the hero away from his purpose, and Cathy Rosier is about as chic as an angel of doom could be. Almost devoid of dialogue, the film owes everything to the subtlety of the acting, the sinister beauty of Henri Decaë's photography and the intricacy of Melville's direction. Action film-maker John Woo claims this movie is nearly perfect, which is probably why he used it as the source for his 1989 thriller *The Killer*. **DAVID PARKINSON**

CAST
Alain Delon *Jeff Costello* • François Périer *Inspector* • Nathalie Delon *Jane Lagrange* • Cathy Rosier *Valerie*

DIRECTOR
Jean-Pierre Melville

SCREENPLAY
Jean-Pierre Melville, from the novel *The Ronin* by Joan McLeod

QUOTE UNQUOTE
I never lose. Never really. **JEFF COSTELLO**

IF YOU ENJOYED THIS, WHY NOT TRY . . .
The Killer (1989)

DID YOU KNOW?
There is no dialogue in the movie for almost the first ten minutes. The first word "Jeff" is spoken by Nathalie Delon at 9.58 minutes.

Who are SECONDS?

The answer is almost too terrifying for words. From the bold, bizarre bestseller. The story of a man who buys for himself a totally new life. A man who lives the age-old dream—*If only I could live my life all over again.*

ROCK HUDSON

In an astonishing change of pace as a Second in

THE JOHN FRANKENHEIMER FILM

SECONDS

A JOEL PRODUCTIONS, INC. PRESENTATION

CO-STARRING SALOME JENS · WILL GEER · SCREENPLAY BY **LEWIS JOHN CARLINO** · BASED ON THE NOVEL BY **DAVID ELY**

PRODUCED BY **EDWARD LEWIS** DIRECTED BY **JOHN FRANKENHEIMER**

Music—Jerry Goldsmith
Produced in Association with Gibraltar Productions, Inc.

A PARAMOUNT PICTURE

Seconds

CERTIFICATE: **X** | YEAR: **1966** | COUNTRY: **US** | **BW** | RUNNING TIME: **105 MINUTES**

SYNOPSIS

A mysterious organisation offers middle-aged banker Arthur Hamilton a metamorphic escape from the boredom of his suburban existence. For $30,000, they will give him a new body and personality, so that he can leave his old life behind and no-one will know that he has been reborn as a "second".

REVIEW

This brilliant social science-fiction movie from 1960s director John Frankenheimer (*The Manchurian Candidate*) was years ahead of its time in both theme and style. A man suffering from a midlife crisis is literally given the chance of a new life. In return for $30,000, a company will provide him with a younger body and personality, and will even arrange for the "death" of his former self. X-rated on its original release and still unavailable on DVD in this country, the frightening premise is intensified by cameraman James Wong Howe's use of stark black-and-white photography and distorting fish-eye lenses. But the most surprising factor in this film's eerie appeal is the strong presence of underrated star Rock Hudson, giving one of his best performances as the deeply disturbed recipient of life-changing plastic surgery, who discovers that his new life might prove too good to be true. **TONY SLOMAN**

CAST
Rock Hudson *Antiochus "Tony" Wilson* • Salome Jens *Nora Marcus* • John Randolph *Arthur Hamilton* • Will Geer *Old man* • Jeff Corey *Mr Ruby* • Richard Anderson *Dr Innes*

DIRECTOR
John Frankenheimer

SCREENPLAY
Lewis John Carlino, from the novel by David Ely

QUOTE UNQUOTE

Death selection may be the most important decision in your life. **MR RUBY**

IF YOU ENJOYED THIS, WHY NOT TRY ...
Face/Off (1997)
Soylent Green (1973)

DID YOU KNOW?
Director John Frankenheimer claimed that every member of the cast and crew, except for himself and Rock Hudson, had been investigated or blacklisted during the McCarthy-era witch hunts.

Se7en

CERTIFICATE: **18** | YEAR: **1995** | COUNTRY: **US** | **COLOUR** | RUNNING TIME: **126 MINUTES**

SYNOPSIS

Veteran detective William Somerset and his rookie partner David Mills discover alarming evidence that links two gruesome murders – a serial killer is punishing those he sees as transgressors, working his way through the seven deadly sins. Unless they catch him, there will be five more killings.

REVIEW

David Fincher's brilliant postmodern *film noir* is a grim and disturbing tale about a vicious serial killer on the loose in an unnamed city, who's murdering his victims in a gruesome manner to atone for the sins he deems them to have committed. After dispatching an overweight man by force-feeding him in the name of gluttony and bleeding to death a lawyer for greed, the killer is now focusing on the five remaining deadly sins – sloth, lust, pride, envy and wrath. There are fine performances from Morgan Freeman as the disillusioned detective, Somerset, who's on the brink of retirement, and Brad Pitt as his enthusiastic rookie partner, Mills, while Gwyneth Paltrow makes a brief though significant appearance as Mills's uneasy wife. Purposely draining his landscapes of colour, Fincher evokes an atmosphere of nightmare proportions as he unfolds a compelling tale of urban terror. **ALAN JONES**

CAST

Brad Pitt *Detective David Mills* • Morgan Freeman *Lieutenant William Somerset* • Gwyneth Paltrow *Tracy Mills* • Richard Roundtree *Talbot* • John C McGinley *California* • R Lee Ermey *Police captain* • Kevin Spacey *John Doe* • Daniel Zacapa *Detective Taylor*

DIRECTOR

David Fincher

SCREENPLAY

Andrew Kevin Walker

DVD EXTRAS

Two-disc edition: commentaries by Brad Pitt, Morgan Freeman, David Fincher (director), Richard Dyer (author), Andrew Kevin Walker (screenwriter), Richard Francis-Bruce (editor), Michael DeLuca (New Line president), Darius Khonjio (director of photography), Arthur Max (production designer), Howard Shore (composer) and Ren Klyce (sound designer); a look at the opening title sequence with commentary by the designers; deleted scenes, alternative ending with commentary; featurette on John Doe's notebooks with commentary; promotional material including theatrical trailer; featurette on the making of the DVD.

CONTENT ADVICE

Contains swearing, violence.

QUOTE UNQUOTE

This isn't going to have a happy ending. **WILLIAM SOMERSET**

IF YOU ENJOYED THIS, WHY NOT TRY . . .

The Horsemen (2009)

DID YOU KNOW?

In the scene where the killer is chased in the rain, Brad Pitt required surgery after he slipped and his arm went through a car window. The accident was kept in the film.

Shadow of a Doubt

CERTIFICATE: **PG** | YEAR: **1942** | COUNTRY: **US** | **BW** | RUNNING TIME: **103 MINUTES**

SYNOPSIS

When Charlie Oakley arrives in the small Californian town of Santa Rosa, he is welcomed with open arms by his sister and her family. However, his teenage niece, who's also called Charlie, soon begins to harbour suspicions about her favourite uncle. Could he be the "Merry Widow Murderer"?

REVIEW

A train, belching out a cloud of ominous black smoke, signifies trouble for a sleepy Californian town in Alfred Hitchcock's own personal favourite of his movies. Joseph Cotten is the man who flees Philadelphia to hide out with his family in their suburban idyll, while Teresa Wright plays his adoring niece and namesake, a pumpkin-pie innocent whose poking around reveals that her suave Uncle Charlie is the suspected "Merry Widow Murderer", wanted for relieving women of their wealth and their lives. Although Hitchcock blurs the line between good and evil (endorsing Cotten's outbursts against the cosy complacency of the town), the two Charlies are inevitably pitched against each other as suspicion increases and the police start nosing around. The movie may lack the show-off set pieces that Hitchcock turned into his trademark, yet its tension never falters. **ADRIAN TURNER**

CAST

Teresa Wright *Young Charlie Newton* • Joseph Cotten *Uncle Charlie Oakley/Mr Spencer/Mr Otis* • Macdonald Carey *Jack Graham* • Henry Travers *Joseph Newton* • Patricia Collinge *Emma Spencer Oakley Newton* • Hume Cronyn *Herbie Hawkins* • Wallace Ford *Fred Saunders* • Edna May Wonacott *Ann Newton*

DIRECTOR

Alfred Hitchcock

SCREENPLAY

Thornton Wilder, Sally Benson, Alma Reville, from a story by Gordon McDonell

DVD EXTRAS

Beyond Doubt: Making of Hitchcock's favourite film; production drawings; art gallery; original theatrical trailer.

QUOTE UNQUOTE

The world's a hell. What does it matter what happens in it? **UNCLE CHARLIE OAKLEY**

IF YOU ENJOYED THIS, WHY NOT TRY ...

Blue Velvet (1986)
The Stranger (1946)

DID YOU KNOW?

The film marked the acting debut of Hume Cronyn, who went on to collaborate with Hitchcock again as an actor in *Lifeboat*, and on the scripts of *Rope* and *Under Capricorn*.

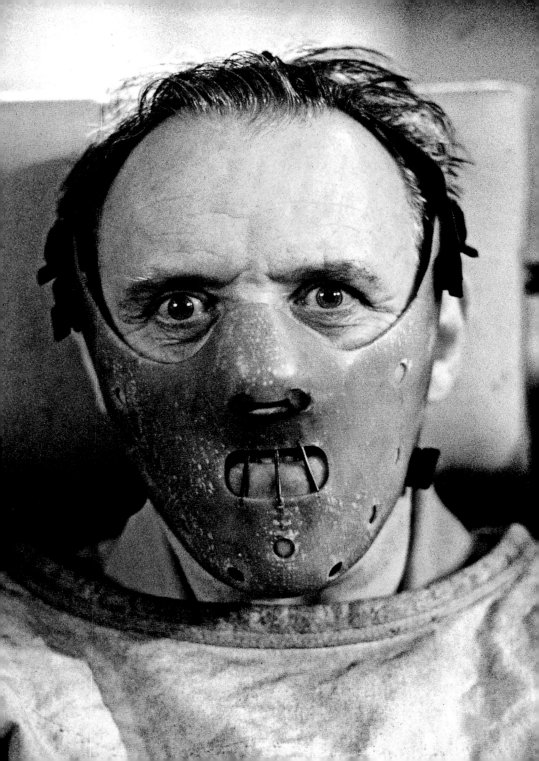

The Silence of the Lambs

CERTIFICATE: **18** | YEAR: **1991** | COUNTRY: **US** | **COLOUR** | RUNNING TIME: **113 MINUTES**

SYNOPSIS

Promising FBI student Clarice Starling is assigned to help in the search for the brutal serial killer known as "Buffalo Bill". She seeks the assistance of Dr Hannibal "the Cannibal" Lecter, a sociopathic former psychiatrist who is being held in a maximum security hospital for the criminally insane.

REVIEW

This multi-Oscar-winning classic, adapted from Thomas Harris's bestseller, gave cinematic serial killers a better image, thanks to Anthony Hopkins's enthralling portrayal of Hannibal Lecter. That Hopkins should collect an Oscar for his role as the crazed cannibal killer was unprecedented, while his "Fava beans and a nice chianti" line became legendary. Jodie Foster also won an Oscar as a fledgeling FBI agent who is drawn into a disturbingly close relationship with Lecter, and it's a testament to her abilities that she holds her own against her scene-stealing co-star. With a track record for directing quirky comedies, director Jonathan Demme (*Married to the Mob*) made a seemingly effortless switch to terror, summoning up a magnificent air of gothic gloom. The hunt for the killer is genuinely suspenseful, but Demme generates the real chill with the probing mind games between his two leads. JOHN FERGUSON

QUOTE UNQUOTE

A census taker once tried to test me. I ate his liver with some fava beans and a nice chianti. HANNIBAL LECTER

IF YOU ENJOYED THIS, WHY NOT TRY . . .

The Bone Collector (1999)
Se7en (1995)

CAST

Jodie Foster *Clarice Starling* • Anthony Hopkins *Dr Hannibal Lecter* • Scott Glenn *Jack Crawford* • Ted Levine *Jame Gumb* • Anthony Heald *Dr Frederick Chilton* • Kasi Lemmons *Ardelia Mapp* • Chris Isaak *Swat commander*

DIRECTOR

Jonathan Demme

SCREENPLAY

Ted Tally, from the novel by Thomas Harris

AWARDS

Academy Awards (5): Film, Director, Actor (Anthony Hopkins), Actress (Jodie Foster), Adapted Screenplay
Baftas (2): Actor, Actress

DVD EXTRAS

Two-disc Definitive Edition: making-of documentaries *The Beginning*, *Breaking the Silence*, *Scoring the Silence*, *Page to Screen*; deleted scenes; outtakes; *Inside the Labyrinth* documentary; photo gallery; trailers; TV spots; trailer for *Hannibal*; Anthony Hopkins phone message. Also available on Blu-ray.

CONTENT ADVICE

Contains violence, swearing, nudity.

DID YOU KNOW?

The movie won the five main Oscars, best picture, director, actor, actress and (adapted) screenplay equalling the achievement held jointly by *It Happened One Night* (1934) and *One Flew over the Cuckoo's Nest* (1975).

Speed

CERTIFICATE: **15** | YEAR: **1994** | COUNTRY: **US** | **COLOUR** | RUNNING TIME: **111 MINUTES**

SYNOPSIS

An extortionist's plan to collect a huge ransom by planting a bomb in an LA skyscraper is thwarted by SWAT daredevil Jack Traven. The devious bomber then challenges Traven with an even more deadly device that's on board a commuter-filled bus and primed to explode if the bus's speed dips below 50mph.

REVIEW

Slipping smoothly into top gear from the nail-biting scene-setting opening, director Jan De Bont's "*Die Hard* on the Buses" moves into the fast lane with a nonstop barrage of brilliantly filmed action, nerve-jangling thrills and death-defying stunts. The casting of *Bill & Ted* airhead Keanu Reeves and the unknown Sandra Bullock was a risky move for the studio in a big-budget action movie, but their good looks, focused performances and chemistry catapulted them into Hollywood's A-list. In support, ever-reliable villain Dennis Hopper provides timely ironic asides that prevent the outrageous plot becoming laughable, and in his directorial debut, former cinematographer De Bont's spot-on pacing keeps the tension and energy levels high. Completely outrageous, over-the-top and as exciting as can be, this wild ride will make you wish your sofa came equipped with seat belts. **ALAN JONES**

QUOTE UNQUOTE

It's a game. If he gets the money he wins, if the bus blows up he wins. **JACK TRAVEN**

IF YOU ENJOYED THIS, WHY NOT TRY ...

Juggernaut (1974)
The Wages of Fear (1953)

CAST

Keanu Reeves *Jack Traven* • Dennis Hopper *Howard Payne* • Sandra Bullock *Annie* • Joe Morton *Captain McMahon* • Jeff Daniels *Harry* • Alan Ruck *Stephens* • Glenn Plummer *Jaguar owner* • Richard Lineback *Norwood*

DIRECTOR

Jan De Bont

SCREENPLAY

Graham Yost

AWARDS

Academy Awards (2): Sound, Sound Effects Editing
Baftas (2): Editing, Sound

DVD EXTRAS

Two-disc Special Edition: commentary by Jan De Bont; specific scene commentary by writer Graham Yost, producer Mark Gordon; three featurettes looking at locations, stunts and visual effects; *HBO First Look* documentary; featurettes on the bus jump and rail crash scenes; interviews with stars and director; five extended scenes; multi-angle stunt sequences; Billy Idol music video; production notes; stills gallery; original theatrical trailers. Also available on Blu-ray.

CONTENT ADVICE

Contains swearing, violence.

DID YOU KNOW?

When director Jan de Bont was working as a cinematographer on *Die Hard*, he got stuck in a lift, and escaped by climbing out of the hatch and jumping onto another lift. His experience formed the basis of *Speed*'s opening seqence.

The Spiral Staircase

CERTIFICATE: **PG** | YEAR: **1946** | COUNTRY: **US** | **BW** | RUNNING TIME: **79 MINUTES**

SYNOPSIS

A murderer stalks a small New England town at the beginning of the 20th century. His victims are all women with some kind of physical disability or frailty; women such as Helen. Mute since childhood, she's a servant in an old, dark Gothic mansion. Her mistress warns her to leave, but is it too late?

REVIEW

Thought-provoking and disturbing, this masterly thriller is directed with touches of sheer genius by Robert Siodmak, who beckons us into a voyeuristic nightmare with taut, creeping camerawork that makes the hair on your neck stand up. However, while this is undoubtedly a classic of 1940s Hollywood Gothic, the movie treads a fine line between acceptable menace and uncomfortable sadism with its story of a serial killer murdering maimed and disabled women. That said, it remains a masterwork, with a fine central performance from Dorothy McGuire as the threatened mute servant working in an old Victorian mansion. With nods to the brooding suspense of Alfred Hitchcock and the unnerving atmosphere of Val Lewton (*Cat People*), this study of an unhinged mind should not be watched alone on a dark and stormy night. **SUE HEAL**

CAST

Dorothy McGuire *Helen Capel* • George Brent *Professor Warren* • Ethel Barrymore *Mrs Warren* • Kent Smith *Dr Parry* • Rhonda Fleming *Blanche* • Gordon Oliver *Steve Warren* • Elsa Lanchester *Mrs Oates* • Sara Allgood *Nurse Barker*

DIRECTOR

Robert Siodmak

SCREENPLAY

Mel Dinelli, from the novel *Some Must Watch* by Ethel Lina White

DVD EXTRAS

The Film Collection: cast biographies; *New York Times* review; photo gallery.

QUOTE UNQUOTE

Helen, I don't want to frighten you... **PROFESSOR WARREN**

IF YOU ENJOYED THIS, WHY NOT TRY ...

The Cat and the Canary (1939)
Mute Witness (1995)

DID YOU KNOW?

Ethel Barrymore, the great-aunt of Drew, was once proposed to by Winston Churchill but turned him down as she thought he did not have much of a future.

Strangers on a Train

CERTIFICATE: **PG** | YEAR: **1951** | COUNTRY: **US** | **BW** | RUNNING TIME: **96 MINUTES**

SYNOPSIS

Playboy Bruno Antony strikes up a conversation with tennis player Guy Haines during a train journey. After a few drinks, Bruno reveals that he hates his father, and empathises with Guy's frustration at not being able to obtain a divorce. His proposed solution? Each bumps off the other's irritant.

REVIEW

This splendid thriller is testimony to Alfred Hitchcock's mastery of technique and his ability to transform even the most unpromising start into a gripping movie. After nearly a dozen writers had turned down the chance to adapt Patricia Highsmith's novel, Raymond Chandler stepped into the breach, only to disagree with Hitch on several key scenes and suffer the humiliation of having his dialogue polished by Czenzi Ormonde, a staff writer. Hitchcock was also underwhelmed by Farley Granger in a role he felt cried out for William Holden. Far more charismatic is co-star Robert Walker (in his final completed role), whose portrayal of a privileged mother's boy is as creepy as it is captivating. And there's fine support from Hitch's daughter, Patricia, as Ruth Roman's sprightly but suspicious sister. The result is a true nail-biter, with the two fairground scenes outstanding. **DAVID PARKINSON**

CAST

Farley Granger *Guy Haines* • Ruth Roman *Anne Morton* • Robert Walker *Bruno Antony* • Leo G Carroll *Senator Morton* • Patricia Hitchcock *Barbara Morton* • Laura Elliot *Miriam* • Marion Lorne *Mrs Antony* • Jonathan Hale *Mr Antony*

DIRECTOR

Alfred Hitchcock

SCREENPLAY

Raymond Chandler, Czenzi Ormonde, Whitfield Cook, from the novel by Patricia Highsmith

DVD EXTRAS

Two-disc Edition: commentary by Peter Bogdanovich, Andrew Wilson and others; preview version of the film; documentary *Strangers on a Train: a Hitchcock Classic*; the victim's point of view; an appreciation by M Night Shyamalan; documentary *The Hitchcocks on Hitch*; 1951 archive newsreel; theatrical trailer.

QUOTE UNQUOTE

Everyone has somebody that they want to put out of the way. **BRUNO ANTONY**

IF YOU ENJOYED THIS, WHY NOT TRY ...

I Confess (1953)
Throw Momma from the Train (1987) ■

DID YOU KNOW?

Hitchcock secured the rights to Highsmith's novel for just $7,500 after bidding for them anonymously.

Straw Dogs

CERTIFICATE: **18** | YEAR: **1971** | COUNTRY: **UK** | **COLOUR** | RUNNING TIME: **116 MINUTES**

SYNOPSIS

Mild-mannered American mathematician David Sumner moves to a small Cornish village with his beautiful English wife, Amy. But the idyllic rural environment has a dark side that explodes into violence. Under siege from the local thugs, David is forced into the ultimate act of retribution.

REVIEW

In this pitch black revenge drama from director Sam Peckinpah, mild-mannered maths teacher Dustin Hoffman finds his manhood tested when he moves to a Cornish village with wife Susan George and encounters local toughs who threaten his home. One of the key movies in the controversial 1970s debate about unacceptable screen violence (it was released in the same year as *Dirty Harry* and *A Clockwork Orange*), this cynical parable virtually states that all pacifists are violent thugs under their liberal exteriors. Reprehensible and disturbing in equal measure, the movie remains potent and shocking, particularly the much-discussed rape scene (the censors were concerned that George's character was unconsciously "asking for it"). Those with a nervous disposition should approach this controversial tale with caution. **ALAN JONES**

QUOTE UNQUOTE

Ok! You've had your fun. I'll give you one more chance! And if you don't clear out now, there'll be real trouble. I mean it! **DAVID SUMNER**

IF YOU ENJOYED THIS, WHY NOT TRY . . .

Assault on Precinct 13 (1976)
Dog Soldiers (2001)

CAST

Dustin Hoffman *David Sumner* • Susan George *Amy Sumner* • Peter Vaughan *Tom Hedden* • TP McKenna *Major Scott* • Del Henney *Venner* • Ken Hutchison *Scutt* • Colin Welland *Reverend Hood* • Jim Norton *Cawsey*

DIRECTOR

Sam Peckinpah

SCREENPLAY

David Zelag Goodman, Sam Peckinpah, from the novel *The Siege of Trencher's Farm* by Gordon M Williams

DVD EXTRAS

Uncut: commentary by Peckinpah biographers Paul Seydor, Garner Simmons, David Weddle; commentary by Katy Haber, dialogue director and Peckinpah's lover/assistant; interview with Peckinpah's biographer Garner Simmons; interview with Susan George; deleted scene; isolated score; information on the deleted scenes (via shooting script & stills); a history of *Straw Dogs* and the British Censor; reprinted letters and memos from the film-makers and the BBFC; on-location documentary from 1971; stills gallery; posters, lobby cards; biographies of Dustin Hoffman, Susan George, Sam Peckinpah, Dan Melnick, Jerry Fielding; US theatrical trailer; US TV spots; US radio spots; trivia, film facts. Also available on Blu-ray.

CONTENT ADVICE

Contains graphic violence, swearing, nudity.

DID YOU KNOW?

One of Sam Peckinpah's famous drinking binges nearly resulted in the collapse of this Cornwall-set shocker. After a night of carousing, Peckinpah wound up in a London hospital with pneumonia. He was only allowed back if he promised to stay off the bottle.

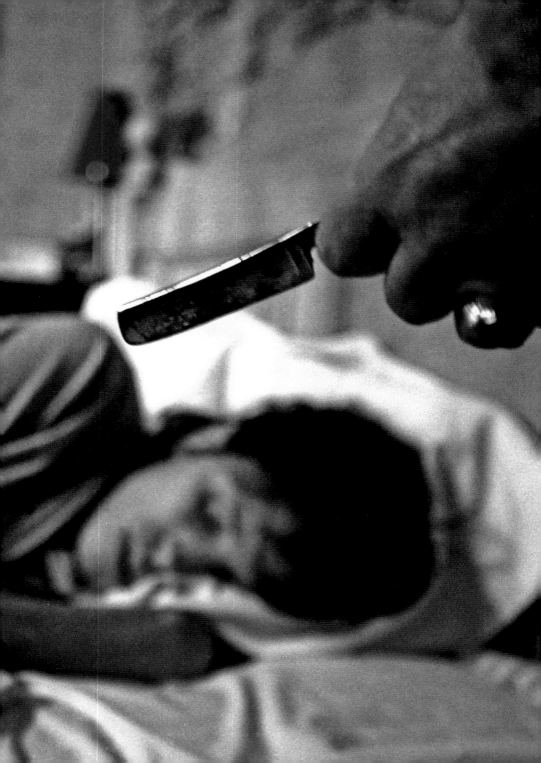

Switchblade Romance

CERTIFICATE: **18** | YEAR: **2003** | COUNTRY: **FR/ROM** | **COLOUR** | RUNNING TIME: **88 MINUTES**

SYNOPSIS

Student Marie accompanies her friend Alex on a summer trip to see her family in their remote farmhouse home. During the visit, a psychopathic intruder enters the property and brutally murders Alex's parents and brother, before abducting the girl in his van. Witnessing the carnage, Marie gives chase.

REVIEW

When French director/co-writer Alexandre Aja called this chiller *Haute Tension* (*High Tension*), he certainly picked the right title. Renamed less aptly for English-language audiences, it's still a nail-biter. There's no anxiety-releasing irony, only seat-edge horror, as desperate student Marie (Cécile de France) tries to rescue her best friend Alex (Maïwenn) from the psychopath who slaughtered her entire family. Though relentlessly gruesome, the feature is more about atmosphere than gore. Every single frame is meticulously composed for maximum effect, while the ultra-glossy production values take it far beyond the realms of the traditional slasher flick. The ultimate twist is pretty unnecessary, but overall this is a terrifying tale that's not easily forgotten. Don't be put off by the subtitles, either – the sparse dialogue makes the film highly accessible. **SLOAN FREER**

CAST

Cécile de France *Marie* • Maïwenn *Alex* • Philippe Nahon *Killer* • Franck Khalfoun *Jimmy* • Andrei Finti *Alex's father* • Oana Pellea *Alex's mother* • Marco Claudiu Pascu *Tom* • Jean-Claude de Goros *Police captain*

DIRECTOR

Alexandre Aja

SCREENPLAY

Alexandre Aja, Grégory Levasseur

DVD EXTRAS

Commentary by Alexandre Aja, Cécile De France; making-of documentary; interviews with cast and crew; interview with special make-up effects artist Giannetto de Rossi; theatrical trailer. Also available on Blu-ray.

QUOTE UNQUOTE

You can't escape from me. **KILLER**

IF YOU ENJOYED THIS, WHY NOT TRY . . .

Psycho (1960)
Wolf Creek (2005)

DID YOU KNOW?

Cécile de France trained with a Thai boxer for two months to get into the right physical shape for her role.

The Taking of Pelham One Two Three

CERTIFICATE: **15** | YEAR: **1974** | COUNTRY: **US** | **COLOUR** | RUNNING TIME: **102 MINUTES**

SYNOPSIS

An ordinary day on the New York underground is shattered when four armed men hijack a subway car and hold its passengers to ransom, demanding $1 million within the hour. A nail-biting situation ensues as the hijackers threaten to start killing the terrified commuters unless the money is paid.

REVIEW

Gerald Greenberg and Robert Q Lovett are the "stars" of this tough and compelling thriller about the hijacking of a New York subway train. As the film's editors, their superb sense of rhythm and pace brings real tension to the radio exchanges between villain Robert Shaw and transport cop Walter Matthau, who tries to prevent Shaw and his gang (known only by their colour codenames) from killing hostages while waiting for the payment of a $1 million ransom. Frankly, the motley collection of clichéd passengers doesn't deserve to be rescued, but, fortunately, director Joseph Sargent keeps the focus firmly on his leads. Shaw is admirably fanatical, and the world-weary, wisecracking Matthau is magnificent. There's also scene-stealing support from Martin Balsam and Hector Elizondo as fellow hijackers, and a catchy score from David Shire. Denzel Washington and John Travolta should have stayed away. **DAVID PARKINSON**

QUOTE UNQUOTE

The guy who's talking's got a heavy English accent. He could be a fruitcake. **LIEUTENANT GARBER**

IF YOU ENJOYED THIS, WHY NOT TRY...

Juggernaut (1974)
The Taking of Pelham 123 (2009)

CAST

Walter Matthau *Lieutenant Garber* • Robert Shaw *Blue* • Martin Balsam *Green* • Hector Elizondo *Grey* • Earl Hindman *Brown* • James Broderick *Denny Doyle* • Dick O'Neill *Correll* • Lee Wallace *Mayor* • Jerry Stiller *Lieutenant Rico Patrone*

DIRECTOR

Joseph Sargent

SCREENPLAY

Peter Stone, from the novel by John Godey

DVD EXTRAS

Theatrical trailer.

CONTENT ADVICE

Contains violence, swearing.

DID YOU KNOW?

The use of colour codenames for the gang members was an influence on Quentin Tarantino, who used the idea for his first movie, *Reservoir Dogs*.

The Talented Mr Ripley

CERTIFICATE: **15** | YEAR: **1999** | COUNTRY: **US** | **COLOUR** | RUNNING TIME: **142 MINUTES**

SYNOPSIS

A chance encounter with a wealthy couple leads to an interesting proposition for penniless Tom Ripley – an all-expenses-paid trip to Europe to bring back their errant son, Dickie Greenleaf. Ripley accepts, but soon finds himself coveting Greenleaf's playboy lifestyle, and envy becomes obsession.

REVIEW

Director Anthony Minghella followed his award-winning *The English Patient* with this absorbing thriller, based on the novel by Patricia Highsmith, which had previously been filmed by Rene Clément as *Plein Soleil* in 1960 with Alain Delon as Ripley. Here Matt Damon plays the young opportunist, charged with seeking out Dickie Greenleaf (an Oscar-nominated Jude Law), the son of a wealthy American shipbuilder who's using his allowance to finance a playboy lifestyle in 1950s Europe. Ripley becomes friends with Dickie, but gradually comes to covet the carefree existence the shipping heir enjoys with his glamorous girlfriend Marge Sherwood (Gwyneth Paltrow). Minghella's classy direction and a superior supporting cast that includes Philip Seymour Hoffman, Philip Baker Hall and Cate Blanchett make this never less than compelling. **LORIEN HAYNES**

QUOTE UNQUOTE

Whatever you do, however terrible, however hurtful... It all makes sense, doesn't it? In your head? You never meet anybody who thinks they're a bad person. **TOM RIPLEY**

IF YOU ENJOYED THIS, WHY NOT TRY ...

The American Friend (1977)
Plein Soleil (1960)   ■

CAST

Matt Damon *Tom Ripley* • Gwyneth Paltrow *Marge Sherwood* • Jude Law *Dickie Greenleaf* • Cate Blanchett *Meredith Logue* • Philip Seymour Hoffman *Freddie Miles* • Jack Davenport *Peter Smith-Kingsley* • James Rebhorn *Herbert Greenleaf* • Philip Baker Hall *Alvin MacCarron*

DIRECTOR

Anthony Minghella

SCREENPLAY

Anthony Minghella, from the novel by Patricia Highsmith

AWARDS

Baftas (1): Supporting Actor (Jude Law)

DVD EXTRAS

Commentary by Anthony Minghella; documentary *Inside The Talented Mr Ripley*; making of the soundtrack documentary; *My Funny Valentine* music video; *Tuo Vu Fa l'Americano* music video; trailers.

CONTENT ADVICE

Contains swearing.

DID YOU KNOW?

Jude Law learned to play the saxophone and Matt Damon the piano for their roles in the film.

The Third Man

CERTIFICATE: **PG** | YEAR: **1949** | COUNTRY: **UK** | **BW** | RUNNING TIME: **101 MINUTES**

SYNOPSIS

Following the end of the Second World War, novelist Holly Martins goes to Vienna on a promise of work from old friend Harry Lime. But when Martins arrives in the city, he is told that Lime is dead and was involved in racketeering. He resolves to clear the man's name but uncovers some disturbing truths.

REVIEW

Developed by Graham Greene from an idea jotted down on the flap of an envelope, this virtually flawless thriller is one of the best British films of all time. Set in postwar occupied Vienna, the plot is a corker, littered with memorable moments – the first appearance of charismatic racketeer Harry Lime; the "cuckoo clock" speech; the climactic chase in the city's sewers – and played to perfection by an unforgettable cast that's led with distinction by Orson Welles as Lime and Joseph Cotten as Lime's friend, second-rate pulp fiction writer Holly Martins. A master of place, angle and shade, director Carol Reed (helped by the Oscar-winning cinematography of Robert Krasker) fashions a city in which menace lurks around every corner, while Anton Karas's jaunty zither music uniquely echoes the wit and drama of this dark yet daringly playful picture.

DAVID PARKINSON

CAST

Joseph Cotten *Holly Martins* • Valli [Alida Valli] *Anna Schmidt* • Orson Welles *Harry Lime* • Trevor Howard *Major Calloway* • Bernard Lee *Sergeant Paine* • Paul Hoerbiger [Paul Hörbiger] *Harry's porter* • Ernst Deutsch *"Baron" Kurtz* • Siegfried Breuer *Popescu* • Erich Ponto *Dr Winkel* • Wilfrid Hyde-White [Wilfrid Hyde White] *Crabbin* • Hedwig Bleibtreu *Anna's "old woman"*

DIRECTOR

Carol Reed

SCREENPLAY

Graham Greene, from his story

AWARDS

Academy Awards (1): Cinematography (black and white)
Baftas (1): British Film

DVD EXTRAS

Two-disc Special Edition: *Shadowing the Third Man* documentary; two US radio plays; feature on Anton Karas; trailers.

QUOTE UNQUOTE

In Switzerland they had brotherly love – they had 500 years of democracy and peace, and what did that produce? The cuckoo clock. **HARRY LIME**

IF YOU ENJOYED THIS, WHY NOT TRY . . .

The Constant Gardener (2005)
M (1931)

DID YOU KNOW?

Orson Welles went missing during some of the shoot in Vienna so assistant director (and future James Bond helmer) Guy Hamilton was used as a stand-in, aided by an oversized hat and a padded coat.

The 39 Steps

CERTIFICATE: **U** | YEAR: **1935** | COUNTRY: **UK** | **BW** | RUNNING TIME: **83 MINUTES**

SYNOPSIS

After a mysterious woman who claims to be a secret agent is killed in his London flat, visiting Canadian Richard Hannay is accused of her murder. Fleeing both the police and an international spy ring, Hannay leads the chase across desolate Scottish moors, while handcuffed to a beautiful blonde.

REVIEW

Alfred Hitchcock brings John Buchan's novel to the screen with characteristic wit and verve, a style he forged in 1930s Britain with this, *The Man Who Knew Too Much* and *The Lady Vanishes*. *The 39 Steps* has all the ingredients of classic Hitch, not least the innocent-man-on-the-run plot, a staple all the way through to 1959's *North by Northwest*. In this case, it's visiting Canadian Richard Hannay (a winning Robert Donat) who gets dragged into an espionage conspiracy after an outing to a London music hall and ends up in Scotland handcuffed to an icy blonde (Madeleine Carroll). Playing "spot the recurring Hitchcock motif" is almost as thrilling as the chase itself, and the chemistry between Donat and Carroll is a rare treat – particularly when they are forced to share a room (quite shocking in 1935). Undoubtedly, this is entertainment of the highest order. **ANDREW COLLINS**

CAST

Robert Donat *Richard Hannay* • Madeleine Carroll *Pamela* • Lucie Mannheim *Miss Smith* • Godfrey Tearle *Professor Jordan* • Peggy Ashcroft *Crofter's wife* • John Laurie *Crofter* • Helen Haye *Mrs Jordan* • Frank Cellier *Sheriff Watson* • Wylie Watson *Memory*

DIRECTOR

Alfred Hitchcock

SCREENPLAY

Charles Bennett, Alma Reville, Ian Hay, from the novel by John Buchan

DVD EXTRAS

Special Edition: documentary on Hitchcock; biographies; behind-the-scenes stills gallery.

QUOTE UNQUOTE

What are "The 39 Steps"? **RICHARD HANNAY**

IF YOU ENJOYED THIS, WHY NOT TRY . . .

The Man Who Knew Too Much (1934)
North by Northwest (1959)

DID YOU KNOW?

In his usual jokey fashion, Alfred Hitchcock handcuffed Robert Donat and Madeleine Carroll together one day and pretended to have lost the key.

Touch of Evil

CERTIFICATE: **12** | YEAR: **1958** | COUNTRY: **US** | **BW** | RUNNING TIME: **104 MINUTES**

SYNOPSIS

Honeymooning in the frontier town of Los Robles, Mike Vargas, special narcotics investigator for the Mexican Ministry of Justice, and his new wife Susan witness a car bombing. They're now mixed up in a case of murder, racketeering and police corruption, in the shape of the unscrupulous Hank Quinlan.

REVIEW

Owing to a misunderstanding between star Charlton Heston and producer Albert Zugsmith, Orson Welles not only appeared in this crime thriller as corrupt, corpulent cop Hank Quinlan, but also ended up directing it. In this way, Welles made the film that virtually capped a style he had helped create: you could say that the span of *film noir* started with *Citizen Kane* and ended with this movie. Originally released by the studio as a co-feature, this has been revealed by time and re-editing to be one of the great American masterworks. It's a deeply disturbing melodrama that pits Welles against Mexican investigator Heston and rivets an audience from its now famed opening title sequence to its grisly finale. The composition, dialogue and characterisations are first-rate – this is what cinema can and should be capable of, and makes for a terrifically entertaining study in depravity. **TONY SLOMAN**

QUOTE UNQUOTE

He was some kind of a man... What does it matter what you say about people? **TANYA**

IF YOU ENJOYED THIS, WHY NOT TRY ...

Red Rock West (1992)
U Turn (1997)

DID YOU KNOW?

While shooting the film, Orson Welles also narrated the trailer for sci-fi staple *The Incredible Shrinking Man.*

The Usual Suspects

CERTIFICATE: **18** | YEAR: **1995** | COUNTRY: **US** | **COLOUR** | RUNNING TIME: **101 MINUTES**

SYNOPSIS

A ship explodes leaving only two survivors, a badly burnt Hungarian and a small-time New York conman. US customs agent Dave Kujan is convinced that a crooked ex-cop masterminded the operation, but the conman has another story to tell – that of five disparate criminals in a police line-up.

REVIEW

Few had even heard of director Bryan Singer or screenwriter Christopher McQuarrie before this movie appeared. Yet, by the end of 1995, it was vying with *Shallow Grave* and *The Shawshank Redemption* for the number one spot in most people's top tens, and Kevin Spacey was suddenly the coolest actor in Hollywood. Was it because it gave the world the criminal mastermind Keyzer Soze? Maybe it was the intricacy of the script and the deft sleights of hand executed by its fledgeling director. Perhaps everyone admired the outstanding ensemble acting. Yes, Spacey fully merited the best supporting actor Oscar for his mesmerising performance, but everyone in that rogues' gallery played their part to perfection, not to mention the mysterious Pete Postlethwaite and confused cops Dan Hedaya and Chazz Palminteri. Whatever the reason, it's a film that demands to be watched again and again. **DAVID PARKINSON**

CAST

Gabriel Byrne *Dean Keaton* • Kevin Spacey *Roger "Verbal" Kint* • Chazz Palminteri *Dave Kujan* • Benicio Del Toro *Fred Fenster* • Stephen Baldwin *Michael McManus* • Kevin Pollak *Todd Hockney* • Pete Postlethwaite *Kobayashi* • Suzy Amis *Edie Finneran* • Giancarlo Esposito *Jack Baer* • Dan Hedaya *Sergeant Jeff Rabin* • Paul Bartel *Smuggler*

DIRECTOR

Bryan Singer

SCREENPLAY

Christopher McQuarrie

AWARDS

Academy Awards: (2): Supporting Actor (Kevin Spacey), Original Screenplay
Baftas (2): Original Screenplay, Editing

DVD EXTRAS

Two-disc Special Edition: commentary by Bryan Singer, Christopher McQuarrie; commentary by John Ottman; *Keyser Soze: Lie or Legend* featurette; three other featurettes; Cannes featurette; *Taking Out The Usual Suspects: Interviews and Outtakes*: Bryan Singer introduces Kevin Spacey and friend, interview with John Ottman; gag reel; US TV spots; trailers with introduction. Also available on Blu-ray.

CONTENT ADVICE

Contains violence, swearing.

QUOTE UNQUOTE

Then he showed those men of will what will really was.
VERBAL

IF YOU ENJOYED THIS, WHY NOT TRY ...

And Then There Were None (1945)
The Last of Sheila (1973)

DID YOU KNOW?

No fewer than five people play Keyser Soze: two of the cast are misleadingly pictured as him; a crew grip plays him as a man with long hair; composer and editor John Ottman played his feet; while director Bryan Singer is Soze's hand lighting a cigarette.

THE
VANISHING
a George Sluizer film

The Vanishing

CERTIFICATE: **15** | YEAR: **1988** | COUNTRY: **NETH/FR** | **COLOUR** | RUNNING TIME: **101 MINUTES**

SYNOPSIS

A Dutch couple, Saskia and Rex, are on their way to France for a cycling holiday. They stop at a service station and Saskia goes inside, but doesn't return. She has vanished. Three years later, Rex is still searching for her and, haunted by the mystery, he will do anything to learn the truth.

REVIEW

Far superior to his own unnecessary 1993 Hollywood remake starring Jeff Bridges and Kiefer Sutherland, this is the original version of George Sluizer's chilling tale of premeditation, abduction and obsession based on Tim Krabbé's novel. As the unassuming family man infatuated with the perfect kidnap, Bernard-Pierre Donnadieu emerges as one of the screen's most chilling, calculating and conceited psychopaths. The quiet satisfaction with which he explains his technique to the victim's boyfriend (Gene Bervoets), three years after she disappeared en route to a cycling holiday in France, is unnerving in the extreme. From the moment we realise Johanna Ter Steege is in danger to the final shocking twist, Sluizer inexorably and expertly draws us deeper into the mystery, exposing our own morbid curiosity in the process. **DAVID PARKINSON**

QUOTE UNQUOTE

You see, Monsieur Hofman, for me dying is not the worst thing. **RAYMOND LEMORNE**

IF YOU ENJOYED THIS, WHY NOT TRY . . .

Breakdown (1997)
Frantic (1988)

CAST
Bernard-Pierre Donnadieu *Raymond Lemorne* • Gene Bervoets *Rex Hofman* • Johanna Ter Steege *Saskia Wagter* • Gwen Eckhaus *Lienexe* • Simone Lemorne [Bernadette Le Saché] *Simone Lemorne* • Tania Latarjet *Denise*

DIRECTOR
George Sluizer

SCREENPLAY
Tim Krabbé, George Sluizer (adaptation), from the novel *The Golden Egg* by Tim Krabbé

DVD EXTRAS
Filmography of director George Sluizer; theatrical trailer; photo gallery.

CONTENT ADVICE
Contains violence.

DID YOU KNOW?
The film was submitted to the Academy Awards as the official Dutch entry for best foreign language film, but was disqualified because of the amount of French dialogue spoken.

Vertigo

CERTIFICATE: **PG** | YEAR: **1958** | COUNTRY: **US** | **COLOUR** | RUNNING TIME: **122 MINUTES**

SYNOPSIS

San Francisco detective "Scottie" Ferguson resigns from the force when his intense fear of heights leads to the death of a colleague. He's persuaded to accept a commission from an old college friend to trail his suicidal wife, only to find himself falling in love with his mysterious quarry.

REVIEW

This Hitchcock thriller was considered a commercial failure on its release, but is now regarded as one of the greatest achievements on film. The Saul Bass opening credits and Bernard Herrmann score unsettle from the start, and Hitch heightens the uneasy atmosphere of his mystery with a vivid colour palette, an unhinged dream sequence and the innovative use of the reverse-zoom shot, which brilliantly conveys his protagonist's debilitating fear of heights. Although Hitch later felt his star was too old for the role, James Stewart succeeds in shattering his all-American Mr Nice Guy persona with a disturbingly dark and complex characterisation, while Kim Novak gives her greatest performance in the demanding dual roles of icy blonde Madeleine and the more earthy Judy. A hallucinatory experience, this remains one of the most painful depictions of romantic fatalism in all of cinema. **TOM HUTCHINSON**

QUOTE UNQUOTE

It just means that I can't climb stairs that are too steep. But there are plenty of street-level bars in this town.
JOHN "SCOTTIE" FERGUSON

IF YOU ENJOYED THIS, WHY NOT TRY . . .

L'Appartement (1996)
Lost Highway (1996)

CAST

James Stewart *John "Scottie" Ferguson* • Kim Novak *Madeleine/ Judy* • Barbara Bel Geddes *Midge* • Tom Helmore *Gavin Elster* • Henry Jones *Coroner* • Raymond Bailey *Doctor* • Ellen Corby *Manageress* • Konstantin Shayne *Pop Leibel* • Paul Bryar *Captain Hansen*

DIRECTOR

Alfred Hitchcock

SCREENPLAY

Alex Coppel, Samuel Taylor, from the novel *D'entre les Morts* by Pierre Boileau, Thomas Narcejac

DVD EXTRAS

Two-disc 50th Anniversary Edition: associate producer Herbert Coleman and restoration team Robert A Harris, James C Katz; *Obsessed with Vertigo* making-of documentary; restoration featurette; *Partners in Crime: Hitchcock Collaborators*; documentary *Hitchcock and the Art of Pure Cinema*; *The Vertigo Archives* featurette; Hitchcock trailer compilation introduced by James Stewart; Truffaut/Hitchcock interviews; production notes.

DID YOU KNOW?

Hitchcock originally wanted his *Wrong Man* actress Vera Miles to star opposite James Stewart, but she had to drop out after becoming pregnant. Miles was back with the director as Janet Leigh's sister in his famed 1960 project, *Psycho*.

The Wages of Fear

CERTIFICATE: **PG** | YEAR: **1953** | COUNTRY: **FR** | **BW** | RUNNING TIME: **130 MINUTES**

SYNOPSIS

Mario and Jo are outcasts living seedy lives in Las Piedras, a small South American town controlled by a foreign oil company. When fire breaks out in an oilfield 300 miles away, they take on the lucrative but potentially deadly job of driving a truckload of nitroglycerin across the mountains.

REVIEW

The tension is unbearable in this nail-biting adventure, as two trucks full of nitroglycerin are driven over 300 miles of inhospitable Latin American terrain in order to help extinguish an oilfield fire. But, for all it says about courage and endurance, this is also a grindingly cynical study of human nature, with each participant willing to sacrifice the others for a bigger payoff. Dramatising Georges Arnaud's novel, director Henri-Georges Clouzot wisely spends time shading in the background detail, which intensifies the excitement of the action by drenching it in a sweaty, anti-Hawksian spirit of rivalry. Unusually winning top prizes at both Cannes and Berlin, this is cinema's most suspenseful condemnation of capitalism, as cinematographer Armand Thirard focuses on the perspiring participants inside their claustrophobic cabs every jolt and bump of the way.

DAVID PARKINSON

QUOTE UNQUOTE

Those bums don't have any union. Nor any families. And if they blow up, nobody will come round bothering me for any contribution. **O'BRIEN**

IF YOU ENJOYED THIS, WHY NOT TRY . . .

Sorcerer (1977)
They Drive by Night (1940)

CAST

Yves Montand *Mario* • Charles Vanel *Jo* • Vera Clouzot *Linda* • Folco Lulli *Luigi* • Peter Van Eyck *Bimba* • William Tubbs *O'Brien* • Dario Moreno *Hernandez*

DIRECTOR

Henri-Georges Clouzot

SCREENPLAY

Henri-Georges Clouzot, Jérome Géronimi, from the novel *Le Salaire de la Peur* by Georges Arnaud

AWARDS

Baftas (1): Film from any Source

DVD EXTRAS

Stills gallery; poster gallery; cast and crew biographies; theatrical trailer; theatrical trailer for *Les Diaboliques*.

DID YOU KNOW?

According to showbiz legend, Yves Montand (who was born Ivo Livi in Tuscany) found inspiration for his adopted French name from a phrase his mother Giuseppina used when he was a child: "Ivo monta!", which means, "Ivo, come upstairs!"

Witness

CERTIFICATE: **15** | YEAR: **1985** | COUNTRY: **US** | **COLOUR** | RUNNING TIME: **107 MINUTES**

SYNOPSIS

Tough cop John Book is assigned to protect Rachel Lapp, a member of the reclusive Amish community, when her son witnesses a murder. Forced to run for their lives, the trio flees to the Lapps' home – a rural refuge unchanged by modern technology and governed by devout pacifist beliefs.

REVIEW

When an Amish boy (Lukas Haas) witnesses a killing and is pursued by the bad guys, he and his widowed mother (Kelly McGillis) are protected by a cop (Harrison Ford), who takes them back to their village to await the killers' arrival. Directed by Australian Peter Weir, it's part love story and part thriller, but mainly a study of cultural collision. This bucolic world is brilliantly evoked: there's a magical barn-raising scene, a beautiful sequence when an embarrassed Ford discovers McGillis in the middle of her ablutions, and a telling episode as the Amish endure the hostility of the tourists who gawp at them. The performances are immaculate, with Ford shining in his first serious dramatic role, and McGillis perfectly cast, the camera adoring her Nordic beauty beneath her bonnet. When the violence does arrive, it seems even more shocking played out on the fields of Amish denial. **JOHN FERGUSON**

QUOTE UNQUOTE

Samuel, the man who was killed tonight was a policeman and it's my job to find out what happened. I want you to tell me everything you saw when you went into the bathroom. **JOHN BOOK**

IF YOU ENJOYED THIS, WHY NOT TRY . . .

The Client (1994)
Leon (1994)

CAST

Harrison Ford *John Book* • Kelly McGillis *Rachel Lapp* • Josef Sommer *Deputy Commissioner Schaeffer* • Lukas Haas *Samuel Lapp* • Jan Rubes *Eli Lapp* • Alexander Godunov *Daniel Hochleitner* • Danny Glover *McFee* • Brent Jennings *Carter* • Patti LuPone *Elaine* • Viggo Mortensen *Moses Hochleitner*

DIRECTOR

Peter Weir

SCREENPLAY

Earl W Wallace, William Kelley, from a story by Kelley, Wallace, Pamela Wallace

AWARDS

Academy Awards (2): Original Screenplay, Editing
Baftas (1): Score

DVD EXTRAS

Interview with director Peter Weir; theatrical trailer.

CONTENT ADVICE

Contains swearing, nudity.

DID YOU KNOW?

In his Amish set thriller, Peter Weir showed he had a sense of humour. Rachel asks Book "you know carpentry?", which was a nod to the fact that Harrison Ford famously earned his living as a carpenter before finding success as an actor.

THE GREATEST THRILLER DIRECTOR

Master of the moment

UNUSUALLY FOR A DIRECTOR, Alfred Hitchcock was as recognisable as any of his leading actors. Through his various TV shows, he cultivated a brand for himself using that famous self-sketched portrait of his jowly profile and the "tiddly-pom" musical theme of Charles Gounod's *Funeral March of a Marionette*. The cinema trailers that he personally hosted for several of his later classics are laced with his uniquely macabre wit. And, of course, he's famous for the many wordless cameos that littered his movies. He contributed 37 appearances to the 50-plus films he made in a career that stretched over five decades, and here they are, in year order, each with the time (in hours and minutes) of his movie moment. JAMIE HEALY

Hitch knew that his image put bums on seats, so he featured it not only on the publicity material but also in the majority of his films

1 *The Lodger* (1926) 0:03 and 1:25
The film Hitch considered his true directorial debut also contains his first cameo. That's him with his back to the camera in a newsroom (and it's fairly likely that he's part of the baying mob near the end). His regular collaborator and partner Alma Reville (they married that year) also appears as "Woman listening to wireless".

2 *Easy Virtue* (1927) 0:21
The director makes only a fleeting appearance in this silent feature based on Noël Coward's play about a divorcee (the now little-known Isabel Jeans) plagued by scandal who marries into a respectable family. He's the dapper chap carrying a walking stick who's on his way out of a tennis court.

3 *Blackmail* (1929) 0:11
Hitch clearly had no qualms about preserving his anonymity after casting himself in his first talkie. He's the man who's continually pestered by a small boy while trying to read a book on the London Underground. This comical interlude is his longest cameo, running for 20 seconds.

4 *Murder* (1930) 1:00
Many of Hitch's appearances amount to little more than a stroll-through during a scene. Here he's walking with a woman past the scene of the crime as amateur sleuths Phyllis Konstam, Herbert Marshall and Edward Chapman plan their next move. Chapman even gives Hitch a look after he departs the frame.

5 *The 39 Steps* (1935) 0:06
Early on in this adaptation of the John Buchan novel, Robert Donat and the mysterious Lucie Mannheim flee from a London theatre after shots are fired. Once outside, they board a bus as bystander Hitchcock nonchalantly throws some litter in the street.

6 *Young and Innocent* (1937) 0:15
An easy one to spot, just after "wrong man" murder suspect Derrick de Marney escapes from the courthouse — Hitch can be seen outside the building, being jostled while holding a camera, as a policeman issues instructions.

7 *The Lady Vanishes* (1938) 1:31
Near the end of the feature, Hitch gives another of his customary walk-throughs. This time it's at Victoria Station. A puff

on a cigarette and cheeky shrug ensure that he doesn't go completely unnoticed.

8 *Rebecca* (1940) 2:01
Hitchcock is only very briefly seen in his American debut. He's walking behind scheming George Sanders and a policeman, as the bobby reprimands Sanders for parking his car illegally.

9 *Foreign Correspondent* (1940) 0:12
Nothing so inhibited in this thriller set on the eve of the Second World War. Hitch takes centre stage, studying a newspaper, as undercover reporter Joel McCrea overhears a doorman greeting diplomat Albert Basserman outside his hotel.

10 *Mr and Mrs Smith* (1941) 0:40
Hitch limits himself to a stroll through the frame for his only out-and-out comedy. There he is, smoking a cigarette as the camera audaciously pulls away from Robert Montgomery's building.

11 *Suspicion* (1941) 0:46
All that walking about was clearly getting a bit taxing. Here he can be spied posting a letter by a parade of shops. This film marked the first of four collaborations between Hitchcock and star Cary Grant.

12 *Saboteur* (1942) 1:01

Exercise is off the agenda again here. Hitch can be seen with a lady friend standing outside the Cut Rate Drugs store in New York, just as the saboteur's car pulls up in front of the building.

13 *Shadow of a Doubt* (1942) 0:15

The cameos take on a more playful edge beginning with this, Hitchcock's favourite of his own films. He appears on the train to Santa Rosa, playing cards with a doctor and his wife, and holding a full suit of spades.

14 *Lifeboat* (1944) 0:25

Ingenuity was required to shoehorn him into the claustrophobic action here — he appears in an advert in the newspaper that William Bendix is reading. He's the "before" and "after" model for "Reduco, the sensational new obesity slayer" that promises "In just four months you too can be slender".

15 *Spellbound* (1945) 0:38

This cameo appearance marks the start of Hitch's obsession with carrying musical instruments — well that's what we assume is in those odd-shaped cases. He's the man coming out of a lift at the Empire State Hotel, holding a violin case and smoking a cigarette.

16 *Notorious* (1946) 1:04

Hitch appears as one of the guests at a party hosted by Nazi spy Claude Rains. He takes a glass of champagne from a bartender and then quickly departs the scene before the arrival of Cary Grant and Ingrid Bergman.

17 *The Paradine Case* (1947) 0:36
Hitch leaves a train station alongside defence lawyer Anthony Keane (Gregory Peck). This time he's carrying a cello case, not that its bulk prevents him from looking cheerful while he takes a puff on a cigarette.

18 *Rope* (1948) 0:01/0:53
Another creative solution was required to slip Hitch into this experimental piece. He can be seen walking along the street during the opening titles (immediately after the credit "Directed by Alfred Hitchcock"), while his famous silhouette likeness is re-created as a neon sign that can be glimpsed through the apartment window later in the film.

19 *Under Capricorn* (1949) 0:03/0:13
In one of his less mischievous outings, Hitch performs the role of jobbing extra. Early in this period melodrama set in Australia, he can be seen wearing a blue coat and brown hat during a military parade in the town square. A little later

on, he's one of the three men on the steps of Government House.

20 *Stage Fright* (1949) 0:38
Less elusive this time, Hitchcock passes drama student Jane Wyman on the street. He turns round and looks slightly puzzled as he overhears her trying to get into character by saying "I'm Doris Tinsdale" as she prepares to impersonate Marlene Dietrich's maid.

21 *Strangers on a Train* (1951) 0:10
Another station, another music case. Just after Farley Granger disembarks in his home town, Hitch boards the train carrying what appears to be a double bass. The scene was directed by his daughter, Patricia, who also co-stars.

22 *I Confess* (1953) 0:01
After the credits roll, the director can be seen strolling through the frame past some steep steps in the city of Quebec, where this tale of a compromised priest (Montgomery Clift) unfolds.

23 _Dial M for Murder_ (1954) 0:12
It was filmed in 3-D, but Hitch only appears in two dimensions. He's in the school-reunion photograph that Ray Milland shows guest Anthony Dawson.

24 _Rear Window_ (1954) 0:25
Wheelchair-bound photographer James Stewart is observing the songwriter's apartment where Hitch appears to be winding up a clock.

25 _The Trouble with Harry_ (1954) 0:21
During the scene when impoverished artist John Forsythe chats in the village store, a trenchcoated Hitch can be seen walking past a parked limousine.

26 _To Catch a Thief_ (1955) 0:10
After suspected jewel thief Cary Grant evades capture by the police, he jumps on a bus and sits down on the back seat. Turning to his left, he gazes (in "I've seen it all now" fashion) at the impassive-looking Hitchcock.

27 _The Man Who Knew Too Much_ (1956) 0:24
Morocco is the setting for the action here. As Doris Day and James Stewart take in the local entertainment, Hitch

can be seen, back to camera, stepping into the frame to watch the acrobats.

28 _The Wrong Man_ (1956) 0:00
It's not strictly a cameo, as Hitchcock appears (albeit in silhouette) as himself, narrating the prologue of this true-life crime drama.

29 _Vertigo_ (1958) 0:10
Having tried strings with a violin, cello and double bass, Hitch turns to brass. Just before James Stewart pays a call on Tom Helmore at his shipbuilding firm, Hitch crosses the screen carrying a horn-shaped case.

30 _North by Northwest_ (1959) 0:02
At the end of the opening credits, as thousands of New Yorkers pack the city streets, Hitch is seen narrowly missing a bus, just after the legend "Directed by Alfred Hitchcock" leaves the screen.

31 _Psycho_ (1960) 0:06
The first and only instance of Hitch dressing up occurs just after Janet Leigh returns to her real-estate firm after enjoying a lunchtime tryst with lover John Gavin. The director is standing on the sidewalk wearing a cowboy hat.

he transfers the infant to his other leg, brushing off his presumably wet trousers.

35 *Topaz* (1969) 0:32
One of the more derided Hitchcocks contains his most memorable appearance. At an airport, the director enters the frame being pushed in a wheelchair. The "invalid" then stands up to greet a man, shaking his hand vigorously.

36 *Frenzy* (1972) 0:03
As politician John Boxer delivers his speech, a bowler-hatted Hitchcock is seen in the crowd and is the only one not applauding. He remains in the throng as the body of a woman is discovered in the Thames moments later. This was the last time the director appeared in the flesh.

37 *Family Plot* (1976) 0:38
The great man bowed out in his final feature in the most recognisable way. No-one can miss that distinctive profile, which is silhouetted through the frosted-glass door of the Registrar of Births & Deaths. We don't know who he's pointing that accusing finger at, but you can bet that foul play is at work. ▪

32 *The Birds* (1963) 0:02
As Tippi Hedren enters the pet shop at the start of the film, Hitch is leaving with two white Sealyham terriers. Named Geoffrey and Stanley, they were so beloved by him that he created the production company Geoffrey Stanley Inc to make his next film, *Marnie*.

33 *Marnie* (1964) 0:04
As Tippi Hedren walks down a hotel corridor with a bell boy, a door opens and Hitch appears. He looks at the departing pair, and then to camera. Talk about breaking the fourth wall.

34 *Torn Curtain* (1966) 0:07
In a fun cameo, Hitch is sitting in the lobby of Copenhagen's Hotel d'Angleterre with a blonde toddler. As if the child has just relieved itself,

Striking the right note

THERE'S NOTHING LIKE A GOOD THRILLER, but the very best tend to have one unifying extra: a superb score that embeds, for ever, the action in the memory. Years after viewing the film, just hearing the evocative music raises goosebumps on the skin as the original feelings of fear or excitement (or a mixture of both) surface again.

From my earliest experiences of screen scores giving me the jitters, two stand out: *Jaws* and *Psycho*. I went to see Steven Spielberg's blockbuster at the cinema on its first release, in the summer of 1975. Even before the death of a naked, night-time swimmer at around the five-minute mark, I was already feeling a bit shaky. There was no doubt something bad was about to happen, a sense of dread was building; I knew she wasn't coming out of the water. And how did I know? There was no shark to be seen, just an underwater point-of-view shot of an unsuspecting skinny-dipper larking about. It was the "something evil this way comes" score from John Williams, booming around the packed auditorium, that sealed her fate.

Look out for the string section! Skinny-dipper Susan Backlinie is stalked by John Williams's unforgettable score

Following that shock opening of the young woman being dragged through the water by an unknown entity, the remaining two hours were an ordeal I shall never forget. Spielberg later admitted that the film would have been only half as effective without that Oscar-winning soundtrack (Williams has now been Oscar-nominated 45 times), particularly as the music could *be* the monster, saving the creature's reveal for later in the movie. Just a few chords are still enough to make me shiver, even now.

My first viewing of Hitchcock's *Psycho* was on TV in the 1970s. I hadn't spoiled things by reading up on the plot beforehand (this was in the days before the internet, and the *Radio Times Guide to Films,* of course), so when Janet Leigh's Marion Crane is butchered about a third of the way in, I was chilled to the core. Obviously, Hitch's magnificently constructed shower scene and the unexpected death of the film's nominal star had a lot to do with it. But much of the horror comes from the music of composer and frequent Hitchcock collaborator Bernard Herrmann (they worked together on seven pictures; if Hitchcock is the "Master of Suspense" then surely Herrmann is the "Master of the Suspense Score"). The menacing strains (played entirely on stringed instruments) burst into a

Brought to Hollywood by Orson Welles, for whom he scored *Citizen Kane* and *The Magnificent Ambersons*, Bernard Herrmann collaborated with Alfred Hitchcock on seven of the master's films, most famously on *Psycho* but beginning with *The Trouble with Harry*

piercing shriek to coincide with the savage slaying. It was murderous fury and screaming agony, both killer and victim. And it did for me; I turned off the television immediately and had to wait until the film came on again a year later before I could get past that terrifying scene.

FOUR OF HERRMANN'S SCORES FEATURE IN THIS BOOK, from *Psycho's* unhinged horror, to the lush crescendos and swirling melodies of *Vertigo*, the exciting urgency of *North by Northwest* and the brutal menace of the 1962 version of *Cape Fear*. And they are all distinctively a Herrmann composition. Indeed, the music for the latter film was so effective that Martin Scorsese had no qualms re-using it when he filmed the remake in 1991 with Robert De Niro. Even Herrmann's work on such non-thrillers as *Citizen Kane, Journey to the Center of the Earth, Jason and the Argonauts* and, his swan song, *Taxi Driver*, would work just as well in a thriller.

NOT ALL MUSIC FOR THE GENRE has to be orchestral. John Carpenter was once touted as the successor to Hitchcock's "Master of Suspense" title, and similarly knows how to use music to enhance pace and mood – the difference is, Carpenter invariably composes the scores himself. The throbbing electronic soundtrack that drives his 1976 siege thriller *Assault on Precinct 13* is not only effectively simple, it's also contemporary. As thrillers moved onto the city's mean streets, going out on location, so the music did, too, plundering popular as well as classical sources.

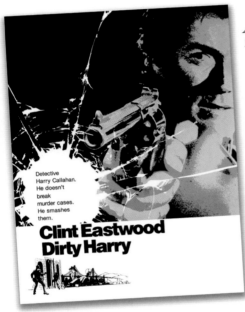

Detective
Harry Callahan.
He doesn't
break
murder cases.
He smashes
them.

**Clint Eastwood
Dirty Harry**

Carpenter freely admits that his *Assault* score owed much to Led Zeppelin's *The Immigrant Song* and Lalo Schifrin's soundtrack to *Dirty Harry* (one of eight Clint Eastwood movies Schifrin would work on). When it comes to a jazz/funk sound, it's also the cool grooves Schifrin composed for *Bullitt* that stand out (ironically, the much-admired car chase sequence wasn't scored). David Shire's groovy theme for *The Taking of Pelham One Two Three* has a 1970s New York vibe that's unmistakeable. It places the film solidly in an era. As does jazz pianist Roy Budd's swaggering theme for the original *Get Carter*.

Music has a unique ability to evoke people and places. I actually prefer the original version of *Touch of Evil* rather than the 1998 Director's Cut (excuse the heresy) because the latter, though closer to Orson Welles's vision, sidelines Henry Mancini's composition that brings to life the sleaze and festering corruption at the heart of a Mexican border town. As *Jaws* was to prove, a soundtrack can do much more than enhance action or signify a character's fate, it can *be* a character. Anton Karas's zither score for *The Third Man* is as much a part of the narrative as Welles's black marketeer. It's called *The Harry Lime Theme*, and it *is* Harry – unsettling yet attractive.

In our selection of greatest scores, the composers are not just writers of music but storytellers. Their refrains are another dimension of cinema, one that holds all the emotion, the horror and the beauty of the images. And without these works of musical genius, the mean and the moody would not be so magnificent. JEREMY ASPINALL

Anton Karas's soaring zither score for *The Third Man* follows Harry Lime (Orson Welles) through the dilapidated streets and shadowy sewers of postwar Vienna

Titles by Decade

Directors

Contributors' Top Tens

DAVE ALDRIDGE
FREELANCE FILM WRITER

1 *Duel*
2 *Falling Down*
3 *Blood Simple*
4 *The Hitcher*
5 *Heat*
6 *A History of Violence*
7 *The Manchurian Candidate*
8 *The Usual Suspects*
9 *The Wages of Fear*
10 *The Yakuza**

JANE ANDERSON
RADIO EDITOR, *RADIO TIMES*

1 *Don't Look Now*
2 *Chinatown*
3 *Jaws*
4 *Psycho*
5 *The Silence of the Lambs*
6 *Rebecca*
7 *Deliverance*
8 *Dirty Harry*
9 *Blue Velvet*
10 *Peeping Tom*

JEREMY ASPINALL
RADIO TIMES FILM UNIT

1 *Jaws*
2 *Chinatown*
3 *The Third Man*
4 *The Night of the Hunter*
5 *Assault on Precinct 13*
6 *Vertigo*
7 *Blue Velvet*
8 *Strangers on a Train*
9 *JFK*
10 *The Limey**

LUCY BARRICK
RADIO TIMES FILM UNIT

1 *Psycho*
2 *The Night of the Hunter*
3 *Peeping Tom*
4 *Les Diaboliques*
5 *Seconds*
6 *Vertigo*
7 *The Manchurian Candidate*
8 *The Wages of Fear*
9 *Point Blank*
10 *Kiss Me Deadly*

DAVID BUTCHER
DEPUTY TV EDITOR, *RADIO TIMES*

1 *The Silence of the Lambs*
2 *Psycho*
3 *Jaws*
4 *Falling Down*
5 *Chinatown*
6 *Westworld**
7 *The Usual Suspects*
8 *Mulholland Drive*
9 *Don't Look Now*
10 *Misery*

ANDREW COLLINS
FILM EDITOR, *RADIO TIMES*

1 *Marathon Man*
2 *Vertigo*
3 *The Conversation*
4 *Jaws*
5 *Blood Simple*
6 *Coma*
7 *Misery*
8 *Get Carter*
9 *The Night of the Hunter*
10 *Chinatown*

GILL CRAWFORD
WRITER, *RADIO TIMES*

1 *Fargo*
2 *The Night of the Hunter*
3 *The Third Man*
4 *The Manchurian Candidate*
5 *Rebecca*
6 *Double Indemnity*
7 *Leon*
8 *Chinatown*
9 *The Parallax View*
10 *Manhunter*

GEOFF ELLIS
WRITER, *RADIO TIMES*

1 *Rear Window*
2 *Chinatown*
3 *Rebecca*
4 *North by Northwest*
5 *Point Blank*
6 *Strangers on a Train*
7 *Don't Look Now*

8 *The Conversation*
9 *Touch of Evil*
10 *The Maltese Falcon*

JOHN FERGUSON
FREELANCE FILM WRITER

1 *Dead Ringers*
2 *Blue Velvet*
3 *Chinatown*
4 *Oldboy*
5 *Get Carter*
6 *Strangers on a Train*
7 *Manhunter*
8 *The Parallax View*
9 *The Third Man*
10 *Best Seller**

TOM FOLLEY
RADIO TIMES FILM UNIT

1 *Chinatown*
2 *Point Blank*
3 *The Conversation*
4 *The Maltese Falcon*
5 *Speed*
6 *Fargo*
7 *North by Northwest*
8 *The Long Kiss Goodnight**
9 *The Bourne Supremacy*
10 *Leon*

SLOAN FREER
FREELANCE FILM WRITER

1 *Don't Look Now*
2 *Peeping Tom*
3 *Dirty Harry*
4 *Repulsion*
5 *The Collector*
6 *The Night of the Hunter*
7 *Se7en*
8 *Manhunter*
9 *Blue Velvet*
10 *Niagara**

RUPERT FROST
FREELANCE FILM WRITER

1 *Vertigo*
2 *Don't Look Now*
3 *The Third Man*
4 *The Usual Suspects*
5 *Les Diaboliques*

* not included in the 100